FIGHTING
MEN
OF THE NORTH

FIGHTING MEN
OF THE NORTH

RONNIE WHARTON

TEMPUS

I'd like to dedicate this book to the two North East boxing academics – John Jarrett and Archie Potts – whose written works on boxing around Newcastle and Sunderland have been absolutely invaluable in compiling this work. John's reviews and fight reports for the bible *Boxing News* have been another particularly vital source over the years.

The author: Ronnie Wharton's interest in boxing came from the radio boxing nights of the early fifties and the broadcasts of commentator Eamonn Andrews and his summariser James Barrington-Dalby. Collecting memorabilia and compiling scrapbooks since those early days led to him putting together a successful series of newspaper articles during the seventies. Continued interest in a series he did for the *Sheffield Star* led to *Boxing in South Yorkshire* being published in 2000 and its companion book *Boxing in Leeds and Bradford* the following year.

Football is his other interest and as well as compiling several handbooks on non-League football for the last twenty years, he has also had his own weekly column on the local football scene in the *Bradford Telegraph* and *Argus*.

Cover photo: Michael Hunter, by kind permission of Les Clark.

First published 2005

Tempus Publishing Limited
The Mill, Brimscombe Port,
Stroud, Gloucestershire, GL5 2QG
www.tempus-publishing.com

© Ronnie Wharton, 2005

The right of Ronnie Wharton to be identified as the Author
of this work has been asserted in accordance with the
Copyrights, Designs and Patents Act 1988.

British Library Cataloguing in Publication Data.
A catalogue record for this book is available from the British Library.

ISBN 0 7524 3551 5
Typesetting and origination by Tempus Publishing Limited
Printed in Great Britain

Contents

Introduction

Outside of London, and along with Liverpool, Newcastle was a hotbed for pugilism in the formative years of glove boxing. The 1868 Marquis of Queensberry's new set of rules was the first step in ending the renowned prize-fight era and, as the nineteenth century ticked to an end, the sport had become respectable and readily accepted by a lot of society. 'Sparring saloons' made a welcome arrival for lads who fancied their chances and there were plenty of chancers in the mining brigade. Music halls and variety theatres provided ready-made venues, the music hall always ready to engage the well-known ringmen in revues. As another sideline, boxers with a bit of pull opened up 'schools of arms' which, besides boxing, often featured fencing, wrestling and physical culture.

The publican at the Percy Cottage in Percy Street in Newcastle, and a fighter himself, Jimmy Lowes was the first name of note in North East boxing. When Lowes found the room above his own public house too small for some of his promotions, he put shows on at Ginnetts Circus (later to become legendary), that, along with the Standard Theatre in Gateshead, became the leading venue in the North. With Newcastle and the surrounding area providing a slice of the top boxers in the country in the shape of Will Curley, George Chrisp and Jack Palmer, the area attracted top drawer Americans. The crowds flocked to see the likes of 'Philadelphia' Jack O'Brien, the coloured champion 'Denver' Ed Martin and the 'Harlem Coffee Cooler' Frank S. Craig. The area had another boost when Dick Burge – one of the most famous boxers in Britain (Burge had challenged George Lavinge for the world lightweight title at the National Sporting Club in 1896) – chose to reside in Newcastle to prepare for forthcoming fights. Will Curley was instrumental in the opening of the St James Hall in Newcastle in 1909 and the 3,000-capacity venue was popular enough to put on two weekly shows for the North East fans.

Boxing lost favour for a while after the outcry by authorities over a proposed fight between the British heavyweight champion 'Bombardier' Billy Wells and the world champion, Jack Johnson, which never took place in 1911. After the First World War, the area's two main boxers, Spike Robson and Johnny Summers (who had actually left the area as a youngster), found fame in London and America.

Author's notes

I do not dispute the fact that the twenty-two boxers featured in this volume would not be every enthusiast's pick of the best boxers to come from the North East. That was not necessarily the exercise. My aim was to include prominent boxers from each decade since the innovation of glove boxing in the last part of the nineteenth century. There are no excuses for the good number of ringmen from the boom years of the thirties and I think boxing historians will agree that the period threw up more characters from the North than in any other boxing era. One point for certain is that Newcastle, and its outlying towns and cities, produced enough quality boxers to fill a second volume and I do not think this book would be complete without mentioning some of them.

Back in the early days, Jarrow's Andrew Tokell claimed the English bantam title before eventually losing to Tom Bowker at the National Sporting Club in 1903. Another lower weight division man was Harry McDermott who hailed from South Shields. Harry claimed the English 7 stone 6 pounds title and, in a career that lasted until 1912, he fought all the top men, including Digger Stanley and Joe Fox. Tom Lancaster of Spennymoor had many big fights around the North East and went twenty rounds with the English welterweight title claimant – the black South African, Andrew Jeptha – at Newcastle. Featured in the classic book *Claret and Cross-Buttock or Rafferty's Prize-fighters* comes Joe Robinson – The Featherweight Champion of the North – while, during the war, another South Shields native, Jimmy Berry, challenged Joe Fox for his British bantamweight title. Sunderland was well represented during the thirties with the Scot Duggie Parker and middleweight Roy Mills. Middlesbrough's Harry Craster hit the headlines in 1939 when he won a disqualification award over the great, unbeaten Frenchman, Marcel Cerdan. Whitley Bay, too, had its own boxing hero, during the inter-war era, in Ginger Roberts who, in nineteen years in the ring and over 150 fights, was never knocked out. Though he became an adopted Yorkshireman, Billy Thompson, the British and European lightweight champion was Sunderland born. Billy beat North Shields' Stan Hawthorne for the vacant British title after Hawthorne, who fought mostly out of Liverpool, had beaten Billy in a northern area title fight. After the Second World War came Sunderland's Northern Area lightweight title holder Hughie Smith and there was also the much-travelled, Jarrow-born, navy man Benny Duffy. Benny eventually settled in Bradford and earned his claim to fame in 1948 when he beat Ronnie Clayton, who was the double Lonsdale Belt holder. The North East had a good heavyweight scene in the late eighties. Glenn McGrory was, of course, the one who landed a world title at cruiserweight, but Hartlepool's Dave Garside, who fought Horace Notice for the heavyweight title, and Newcastle's John Westgarth both stopped him. Paul Lister and Stewart Lithgo, who landed the Commonwealth cruiserweight title in 1984, were not far behind in the same weight division. Moving into the new century there was a performance of guts to rival many of the area's great performances from the past when, in keeping with the tradition of Hartlepool ring battlers, Kevin Bennett landed the Commonwealth lightweight title with a points win against Michael Muya at Bridgend Recreation Centre.

Will Curley

While it is probably fair to say that Jimmy Lowes certainly did as much as anyone to establish the fight game in the North East, George Chrisp and Will Curley were the two fighters who took the gloved sport into its next era. Chrisp claimed the British title in 1897; two years later Will Curley was fighting for the world title in New York against one of boxing's legends. A sensational first-round victory over the British champion followed, and when his career started to come to a close, Curley took over promotional activities at the famed Newcastle venue, Ginnetts Circus, and then was instrumental in the opening of the city's major boxing hall – St James Hall – in 1909.

Born in Newcastle in August 1876, Will Curley learnt to fight on street corners during his time as a juvenile paper seller. Competition was rife and a youngster needed plenty of guile to prevent others from pinching his pitch. Sneaking into public houses, where contests were often held in spare rooms, the thin, pallid youngster developed a hunger to compete in the ring. The way forward in the early days was to enter the various open competitions and improve enough to get a backer. Weighing only 6 stone 8 pounds at sixteen years old, young Curley tried to enter a flyweight competition fixed at 7 stone 6 pounds. Jimmy Lowes, a fighter himself and a focal point for the sport in the Geordie capital, ran shows in a room above the Percy Cottage pub. Proprietor Lowes went round to see Will's mother and was told her lad always wanted to fight somebody. Thinking the first punch on the nose would cure him, she told Lowes to let him have a go. The mother's prediction didn't come true. Curley won the competition and, thereafter, entered and won others. Once he had bettered the local fighters and his name had spread, fighters from other parts of the country came to pit themselves against him. His performances saw his name at the top of the bill and, in his first four years as a fighter, the only lad he could not beat was Tommy Murphy. The pair boxed a draw and became friends. Tommy became his trainer and sparring partner. His first defeat was suffered in 1896, when Gateshead rival Charlie Beadling beat him over twenty rounds. Curley soon got over the setback when he stopped Londoner Ted Daley in his next fight and, when another fighter from the capital ventured north, Will out-pointed Tom Turner over twenty rounds in a fight arranged for the 8 stone 3 pound English title.

Americans were already appearing in British boxing halls and the Newcastle-born lad gained a twenty-round win in a 16ft ring over visitor Pat Haley (who would later step in with the likes of Terry McGovern and Abe Attell), at the Standard Theatre in Gateshead in 1897. Curley's pedigree shot higher when he stopped Australian Billy Murphy in thirteen rounds. Murphy had knocked out Ike Weir in fourteen rounds in San Francisco for the world featherweight title, though the claim wasn't taken seriously in America. Efforts were made to get the backing for a British title fight when an offer came from America to fight for the world featherweight title.

George Dixon, a black man known throughout his carer as 'Little Chocolate', was born in Halifax, Nova Scotia, and in a ring career lasting twenty years, was reputed to have made around 800 ring appearances. His manager, Tom O'Rourke, told the story that he regularly fought fifteen times a week in the dance halls and theatres throughout America with the often-made promise that the Negro would pay a forfeit if his opponent lasted longer than four rounds. Nat Fleischer, boxing's great scribe, though he never saw him box, rated the 5ft 3in, 8 stone 8 pound Canadian Negro above the greatest of ring artists such as Abe Attell, Jimmy Wide, Jim Driscoll and Benny Leonard. A ferocious puncher with both hands, Dixon's specialist punch was a double left lead to the body. 'Little Chocolate' had been over to London to beat Nunc Wallace for the world bantamweight championship in 1890 and had followed that by winning the world featherweight title in 1892 when he knocked out Jack Skelly in New Orleans. He retained the title until 1897, when he lost to Solly Smith in San Francisco before regaining his title from Dave Sullivan a year later. English fighter Ben Jordan had out-pointed Dixon in the United States in July 1898 and laid claim to his title (although in fact Dixon didn't regain his title until four months after his fight with Jordan).

The fight between Curley and Dixon was held in the Broadway Athletic Club in New York on 2 November 1899. Curley was a match for everything Dixon tried and the Newcastle man even out boxed the American-based Canadian at times. By the twelfth round the fight looked to be over for Curley. Dixon threw a left swing followed by a right to the jaw, which floored the British challenger. The bell sounded before the count finished and cornerman Murphy had to carry Will to his corner. Murphy managed to get his man out for the next round and Curley surprised the American audience by withstanding the onslaught. His British bulldog tenacity carried the fight the full distance. Dixon won the fight but looked the worse for wear with a badly damaged left eye. The big reception was for the gallant loser.

Two months afterwards, in his first fight in the new century, Curley was boxing in front of his own crowd at Ginnetts Circus (the building was in Northumberland Street and the name came from a lion tamer who staged all sorts of shows at the venue). Will's opponent was another London fighter and the stakes were for a £250 purse plus side stakes of £200 over twenty rounds

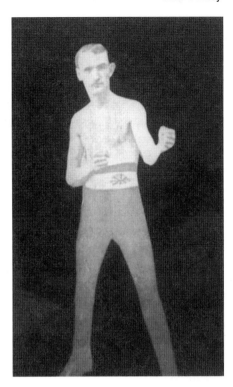

Will Curley, star of Ginnetts Circus and
instrumental in the opening of Newcastle's famous
venue, St James Hall.

using four-ounce gloves. Paddington's Nat Smith gave Curley a great fight and it
needed a strong finish from the local man, who put Smith down twice in round
nineteen, to ensure a home win.

The win guaranteed approval from the National Sporting Club who decided to
give the twenty-five-year-old North-Easterner a crack at the title. In the meantime,
Curley's next opponent at Ginnetts Circus, three months later, was Birmingham's
Jabez White who had made his name by beating the American, Mike Sears, in 1897.
In his previous fight, White had beaten Harry Greenfield at the Sporting Club in a
bout that contested the 9 stone 2 pound championship of England (the lightweight
title was vacant at the time, as Dick Burge had relinquished it). The fight with Curley
was fixed at 9 stone 1 pound and, while Curley had no problem at the weight, White
had to come down. There was a big Birmingham presence at the Circus and, while
waiting for the gong to start the bout, White's broker invested £100 on his man. Two
minutes later the money had gone. White had come out of his corner breezing with
confidence and peppering Curley with his left. Will had been forced to concentrate
on his defence, but when the Newcastle man suddenly moved his head to the right,
White's left went over Curley's shoulder. Curley quickly countered with a left hook
and the place was in uproar. The pole-axed champion never moved a muscle. It was
the first and last time Jabez White had been knocked out

In January 1901, Curley made his debut at the National Sporting Club against
one of the club's big favourites, Jack Roberts, who hailed from Broadstairs in

Kent. Roberts had fought over twenty times at the famous club. Not the best skilled boxer in the game, the thick-set Roberts was known for his stamina and ability to take punishment – assets that would serve him well against the Newcastle man. With the title vacant after Ben Jordan's retirement, the fight for £125 plus a side stake of £200 was for the English 9 stone title. Because of his demolition of Jabez White, ringside betting made Curley the 9-4 favourite. Although if experience was to be a factor, the twenty-eight-year-old Roberts had taken part in four times as many fights. From the outset, Curley dished out a boxing lesson. Roberts just could not cope with his speed. Completely outclassed, only his capability of soaking up the excessive punishment kept Roberts in the fight. The crowd had seen Roberts take a hiding before, but not like this, and the odds shot up to 20-1. Will put his man down in round four but somehow Roberts managed to rise and hang on until the bell. With nothing coming back, Will hit him all around the ring in the next round.

By now the onlookers were shouting for a stoppage. One ringsider offered a thousand pounds to a cigar on Curley. Ring patron Lord Lonsdale took the bet, as Curley went out to finish the job. In absolute desperation, Roberts managed to land a counter and to the complete amazement of everyone present, it was Curley's turn to go down, rise and hang on until the end of the round. Roberts was staggering again in the next round, but came off the ropes and caught Curley with a swinging right. Will toppled and, as he rose again, he saw Roberts' punch coming but could not evade the finishing blow. On the brink of defeat Roberts had pulled the fight out of the fire.

Three months later, Roberts took part in a fight that so affected him that, although he fought till he was thirty-seven years old, he only won thirteen out of his last thirty-eight fights. His opponent that day, Billy Smith, in a fight for the English featherweight title, was knocked out in round eight and never regained consciousness. He died in hospital two days later. Jack had to stand trial, but after Lord Lonsdale had spoken on his behalf and the court accepted that the fight was held under the auspices of the National Sporting Club, Roberts was cleared of any possible manslaughter charges. He lost his title to Ben Jordan, who had returned from retirement to knock Jack out in five rounds.

When the rematch with Curley came in February 1902, this time in Newcastle, Will knocked Roberts out in three rounds. Curley's last few fights were around Newcastle and one of the best remembered was an eight-round knockout over Pedlar Palmer in a match fought at 8 stone 12 pounds. Curley started promoting shows himself at Ginnetts Circus and, in the years leading up to the First World War, he became as well known in the new role as he had been as a fighter. When Ginnetts Circus was refused a licence renewal, Curley, with the help of the Baker family, decided Newcastle needed a custom-built boxing hall. The site chosen was near the football ground and St James Hall opened for business in 1909. The North-East pioneer of the sport remained around the boxing scene for quite some time and died, well into his nineties, in 1973.

George Chrisp

American fighters have always been popular on this side of the Atlantic and, in the years leading up to the start of the twenty-first century, middleweights going on heavyweights, Frank S. Craig (the 'Harlem Coffee Cooler') and 'Philadelphia' Jack O'Brien, strode through England exploiting the gap between the two fighting countries. One of the few British boxers to stand up to the pair for any length of time was Newcastle ringman George Chrisp (sometimes referred to as Crisp). Born in the Geordie capital in 1872, and a contemporary of Will Curley, Harry McDermott and Jack Palmer, Chrisp had come to prominence after winning several money fights in his native North East. Although he was not much above a welterweight, like many others of his era, stepping up to fight heavyweights was never a problem.

When the National Sporting Club failed to get a middleweight title fight between John O'Brien (out of the game through illness) and Ted Pritchard (not in training either) off the ground, the club organised an eight-man knockout competition for the English middleweight championship belt. A different Jack O'Brien (a Welshman, not to be confused with Philadelphia Jack) had claimed the English title after a win over Alf Mitchell in 1891. Pritchard had lost his claim to the title after a defeat by the Australian Jem Hall who had since returned to Australia enabling Pritchard to renew his claim. The winner of the competition was Ted White who had come to note after his ABA heavyweight title win in 1887. White had in fact entered the 10 stone competition, but was found to be too heavy, and so switched to the heavyweight class to become the lightest winner ever. The best scrap en route to White's triumph had been his three-round bout with Chrisp. The Newcastle man found the backing to challenge White and the Sporting Club fully agreed to promote the fight for the title.

This was George's first big fight in London and, although the result was never in any real doubt, it took White the full twenty rounds to beat the Newcastle man, who won praise from the knowledgeable crowd for never giving up trying. Returning to his North-East roots he beat, among other locals, Jack Thompson and Johnny Robinson. Over the next year he dropped a decision in London to Jerry Driscoll and was stopped in seventeen rounds in Newcastle to the American Charley Johnson (who died in 1902 at thirty-one years of age).

During 1898 he drew with, and also beat in just one round on a disqualification, the former world welterweight champion, 'Mysterious' Billy Smith. In February 1897, Chrisp had met one of those notorious fighters of the era in Jem Smith. Now approaching his mid-thirties Smith linked the backend of the bareknuckle days to the early days of the glove fighting period. Jem, whose fights hit the headlines for the unruly incidents that happened at them, never liked gloves and was always more at home with the 'raw 'uns'.

Born in 1883, Smith came from the tough St Luke district of central London and had proved himself in street fights before winning novice competitions. Former prize-fight champion, Jack Knifton, saw enough to mould him into a champion at London Prize Rules and like most of the old bareknuckle fighters Smith cultivated a band of followers. Unfortunately Smith's fondness for drinking and betting saw him court an unruly crew who made their presence felt strongly at his fights and more than once influenced the result of the contest. The prize-fights were coming to an end in England, and so, to avoid confrontation with the authorities, fights were arranged in secret locations across the Channel. Smith's most famous fight took place in France in 1888, when he fought the Irishman who went on to find fame in America, Jake Kilrain. The fight lasted two-and-a-half hours and 106 rounds with Smith going down thirty-six times. Fading light helped bring the fight to a conclusion and Smith's band of ruffians helped sway the decision to call a draw. Smith didn't fight again for two years but then returned to seal the British title with a ten-round win over former wrestler Jack Wannup. Next came his two big fights with the famous Australians Peter Jackson and Frank Slavin. Jackson had too much ring craft for Jem. The aborigine giant outclassed him from the start and, in the final round, an upset Smith threw his man from a wrestling hold to earn a disqualification. Smith wanted to continue with bare knuckles but the police, who were present throughout, intervened. The bareknuckle fight with Slavin was held in Brugge, Belgium, where Smith's hooligan supporters used sticks and knuckledusters against the Australian to make sure their man got his undeserved draw.

Jem and Ted Pritchard had been at loggerheads for years since Jem had been one of the ruffians who had invaded the ring to influence the referee in one of Pritchard's fights. Smith and Pritchard met for the title in Jack Wannup's gymnasium. Pritchard took Smith's title in three rounds. The return, four years later, was a fiasco. Jem regained his title, but the circumstances in which he beat Pritchard in two rounds left a lot to be desired. Smith hit Pritchard when he was down and then his team of ruffians held the rope in such a way that Pritchard could not get up.

Dick Burge challenged Smith for his title, but the lighter man could not make the weight difference count and then Smith lost his crown to the visiting New Zealander, Dan Creedon, who finished Jem off in two rounds at the National Sporting Club. Creedon returned home and Smith put a claim back on his title.

George Chrisp, the Newcastle fighter who took on the leading fighters of the USA.

Now thirty-four years of age, Smith's next fight was a trip to Newcastle to face Chrisp. The boastful Smith had stated to the press that he would take care of Chrisp inside of eight rounds. There was great interest in the fight. There were also plenty of fighting colliers to take up their man's cause if Smith's followers, who like Jem were getting a little long in the tooth, started misbehaving. Smith was thirty-four pounds heavier, but was soon to be seen as a spent force. Chrisp's punching was too much for the old champion; in five rounds Chrisp had claimed his first title.

Later that year, George beat the Australian, Edward 'Starlight' Rollins, on a twelfth-round disqualification at Newcastle's Olympia and, into 1898, Chrisp knocked out Jim Richardson at the Standard Theatre Gateshead.

Nicknamed the 'Harlem Coffee Cooler', the American Frank S. Craig, with his perpetual beaming face, was one of the most popular visitors to English rings. His acceptance, as a Negro, in Britain during this period of boxing history was in sharp contrast to what was happening within his own country. There were exceptions, though, and boxers like Joe Gans and George Dixon became world champions in a period when it was really difficult for coloured fighters. Some found work in Britain, but Paris, in particular in the years around and after the First World War, was a haven for good American coloured fighters. Born in New York in 1870, Craig arrived in Britain in the summer of 1894. Most of his early fights had been in his home city and in Philadelphia and, prior to his visit to Britain, he had lost to Peter Maher and Dan Creedon. In his first fight in

England, he beat John O'Brien in two rounds at the Sporting Club to claim the British middleweight championship – a title he strengthened with a two-round win over Alf Mitchell and a one-round knockout over Ted Pritchard, who many considered the legitimate champion. His popularity was such in London that in November of the same year he fought fourteen times in twenty-five days with the majority of his fights not going for more than one round.

He was matched against the top Australian heavyweight Frank Slavin but was unable to cope with conceding a couple of stones in weight to one of the leading heavyweights of the time. Slavin finished the American in the first round. New Zealander Dan Creedon arrived in the country and repeated an earlier victory: out-pointing Craig over twenty rounds to take his title. The title was soon in disarray again when Creedon left the country. Fellow American, Dick O'Brien, arrived and proved Craig was human by knocking him out in two rounds at the Olympic Club in Birmingham. So when Craig met Chrisp, in November 1889, some reports relate that the fight was for the English middleweight title that Dick Burge was now claiming after a disqualification win over Dick O'Brien. Other publications, however, state that the fight was for the English heavyweight title: a title that George, having beaten Jem Smith, did have within his grasp. It took the 'Coffee Cooler' thirteen rounds to end the resistance of George Chrisp, but when Craig left to try his luck back in America for a year, it left the door open again for other claimants for both titles.

Dido Plumb, who had fought for the title against Ted White in 1896, claimed the middleweight title and then, in 1901, Chrisp beat Ben Taylor in eight rounds at Gateshead to sanction his right to the English heavyweight title. However, his title reign would be short-lived, with the arrival of another American to British shores. The new arrival's fighting name, 'Philadelphia' Jack O'Brien, suggests an Irish background. Although Jack – real name Joseph F. Hagan – was born in Philadelphia, his parents were from County Derry. His career would be later clouded in controversy, when he signed a statement showing the majority of his fights, including championship matches, had been fixed. In 1901 he spent a year in Britain, where no one could touch him, laying claim to both the English middleweight and heavyweight titles. Odds were 3-1 on O'Brien when the American travelled north to take the local man on at Ginnetts Circus. G.T. Dunning, of the *Sportsman* publication, refereed the contest. A stone heavier, George had backed himself, financially, to go ten rounds with the 5ft 10½in middleweight challenger. The American damaged and closed one of Chrisp's eyes early on and, to win his money, the Newcastle ringman was forced to box from a distance.

Chrisp did well to hang in, and when he started to trade punches with the visitor, the big crowd went wild. O'Brien was always the more convincing and, in round eleven, he had Chrisp helpless. A barrage of lefts and rights saw the action go towards the ropes, before a textbook left hook finished off the Newcastle man.

O'Brien ran up a number of easy victories in the north and Scotland and a seven-round win over Frank S. Craig at the National Sporting Club before he set sail for America with a total of eighteen wins from his British tour. But George Chrisp's championship career was over. There was still mileage left in his body and he boxed at Ginnetts Circus until the demise of the famous venue. But with more defeats than wins, the latter years of his career were insignificant.

Jack Palmer

The 'Pitman's Champion' Jack Palmer, who hailed from Benwell just outside Newcastle, was another North-East lad who had learned the rudiments of his art in Jimmy Lowes' pub in Percy Street. Real name Liddell, Jack changed his name to Palmer so as not to be confused with his three siblings who also liked to duck under the ropes in Jimmy's hostelry to earn two bob for going three rounds (rounds were only one minute long). With the majority of the competitors and onlookers being miners, it was a tough learning centre for any aspiring youngster. His first recorded win was in a four-rounder over Gateshead's Jack McGurk. Appearing at the Standard Theatre in Gateshead was a step up from Jimmy Lowes' pub and his first important win was at Ginnetts Circus, when he defeated Londoner Jack Farley over eight rounds in March 1900.

Later in the year came the 'Pitman's Champion' title fight with Wrekenton's Jack Mullen at Gateshead. Jack was out-pointed over twenty rounds, but the crowd refused to accept the decision. There had to be a rematch and, when it came in the following year, Jack made sure the result was beyond dispute when he knocked Mullen out in round fifteen. Wins over Lachie Thompson and Harry Barnett followed before he met Jack Scales in Newcastle in 1901. Scales had met 'Philadelphia' Jack O'Brien in Newcastle the previous month and Palmer fancied his chances against the heavyweight who had first come to fame by winning a competition in London in 1899. A year later Dick Burge brought Scales down to earth when he flattened him in one round in a contest for the English middleweight title. Things went wrong for the local man in round eleven when Scales put him down. It looked like the big money was on Scales because the quick count, which ended Jack's challenge, was reputed to have been only of about five or six seconds duration. Scales couldn't handle the American visitors of the era: later in the year, Kid McCoy put him down in one round (Jack was one of three McCoy victims on the same night) and O'Brien did him again, this time in one round. Scales claimed the British heavyweight title after he knocked out Ben Taylor for the 1902 Coronation Championship Belt. Defending his title against Harry 'Slouch' Dixon at the National Sporting

Club, he lost his title claim when Charlie Wilson beat him in three rounds before the end of the year.

The Philadelphian, Charles McKeever, who had twice fought 'Mysterious' Billy Smith for the world welterweight title in New York before the turn of the century, losing the first fight after twenty-five rounds and drawing the second meeting over twenty, arrived in England in the summer of 1900. It was a period when the English titles were open to all comers and McKeever claimed the English middleweight title with a fifteen-round win over Dido Plumb at the Sporting Club. The Newcastle fighter got his chance with McKeever at Ginnetts Circus and the affair lasted less than two rounds. Egged on by his fervent and almost delirious supporters Jack continually fouled the American. With McKeever not averse to using his own rough tactics, it was the crowd's antics, playing their own part in the action, which brought affairs to an unsatisfactory conclusion. After fighting broke out in the crowd, the referee decided his only alternative was to halt proceedings and record a no-decision bout. The pair was matched again and McKeever returned to the lion's den in Newcastle to beat Jack in twelve rounds. In January 1902, 'Philadelphia' Jack O'Brien beat McKeever in three rounds in the capital, before both fighters returned to America. Jack claimed his right to the title and strengthened that claim by knocking out Dave Peters in seven rounds in Merthyr.

Eddie Connolly had fought in England five years earlier, defeating Dick Burge at the Olympic Club in Birmingham and knocking out Tom Causer in a fight billed as the 132-pound world championship decider. The Canadian had claimed the world welterweight title with a victory over Matty Matthews in New York in 1900, although his reign was short-lived: James Rube Ferns succeeded to his title two months later. In his first fight on English soil since 1897, Connolly out-pointed the Irishman Pat Daley at the National Sporting Club. Jack Palmer was his next opponent. Palmer rose to the occasion and out-pointed the Canadian in Newcastle. With the Sporting Club keen to hold the rematch, Jack made his debut at the headquarters of boxing. Palmer reached his pinnacle in British boxing by stopping Connolly in seven rounds. Later in the year, when a second rematch was secured, Jack completed a hat-trick by out-pointing the Canadian over fifteen rounds.

Still a growing lad, at just under 6ft tall, Palmer moved to the heavyweight division and took part in what is often cited as the first Queensberry Rules heavyweight title match, in March 1903, in front of loyal supporters at Ginnetts Circus. His opponent was a twenty-one-year-old Londoner called Ben Taylor. Nicknamed the 'Woolwich Infant', Taylor had begun fighting in a travelling booth in 1900. The Londoner weighed around 14 stone, considerably more than Palmer, whose regular fighting weight was only a few pounds over 11 stone. Born Frederick Thomas, but called Ben after the famous London clock, Taylor relied on strongman tactics to win his fights. He carried a reputation of refusing to train and work on his weaknesses, which became apparent if he failed to finish his man by brute strength. He had joined the big league after a successful three-round trial with Jack Scales at the National Sporting Club. Scales had knocked

Jack Palmer, the North-Eastener who challenged Terry Burns for the world heavyweight title.

him out in ten rounds for the Coronation Championship Belt in June 1902 and, two months before he came to Newcastle to fight Palmer, he had drawn over thirteen rounds with Harry 'Slouch' Dixon at the London venue, Wonderland (the fight had gone thirteen rounds because the referee was unable to make up his mind as to who had won). Taylor had ventured north before when he lost to George Chrisp in two rounds at the Standard Theatre Gateshead in 1901.

It was the ideal match for the working man on a Saturday night and interest in the fight was immense; those who were unable to get in had to wait outside to hear news. Those who were lucky enough to witness the action saw a one-sided affair, with Palmer bringing his followers to their feet by flooring Taylor eight times for short counts. The end was inevitable and it came with a right to the chin in round eight.

Taylor had more losses than victories, because he refused to take the fitness side of the business seriously. Instead he preferred to spend his occasional winnings on a drinking spree. But Taylor found lasting fame in 1908: he became the first Englishman to fight visiting American heavyweight legend Jack Johnson in England. When Johnson, stopping in the country en route to Australia chasing world champion Tommy Burns, decided to take the fight seriously, the canvas trips reached double figures.

Poor Ben's life ended tragically at only thirty-five years of age. He never came home from a Boxing Day night out and was found dead the following morning. The verdict given was 'murder by some person or persons unknown'.

There was little time for resting on laurels, for London wanted to look at the new heavyweight king. Jack was invited to box at the National Sporting Club, and only three weeks after his win over Taylor, he could not have had a tougher opponent than the American, Jack 'Twin' Sullivan. The fight was for the English middleweight title, which, in theory, Palmer still held despite moving up to contest the heavyweight title. Palmer came in at 11 stone 10 pounds to Sullivan's 10 stone 13 pounds. Will Curley, who had made sure Jack was in peak condition by training him at Whitley Bay, was in Jack's corner. Sullivan's twin brother Mike, who would twice challenge Joe Gans for his world welterweight title in 1906 and then claim the title when Gans moved back to lightweight, was in the American's corner. A hard, vigorous contest was recorded as a draw, a result that was well received by the more reserved Sporting Club audience, but not accepted by either fighter. Then it was back to Ginnetts Circus for his next big challenge. The Geordie knew all about the coloured American, Frank S. Craig, the 'Harlem Coffee Cooler'. He had knocked George Chrisp out in thirteen rounds for the same title in 1897 and fought in Newcastle the previous summer only for fellow American 'Denver' Ed Martin to knock him out twice in short rounds in fights which were claimed to be for the same title. Though he was around until after the war, Craig was starting to slip, and Palmer gained revenge for Chrisp by beating Craig over twelve rounds.

By now he was much in demand further afield and the Benwell heavyweight accepted an invitation to box in South Africa. He became that country's middleweight champion in beating Jack Lalor over twenty rounds at Wanderers Hall in Johannesburg, but he lost his second fight, for the South African heavyweight title, to Mike Williams at the same venue. A hard shot to the solar plexus put Palmer down in round two. Three more counts followed, but the Newcastle man refused to give in until he had no choice in round eight. The South Africans were much impressed by Palmer's bravery against a much heavier opponent in his eight-round defeat, and when he arrived back in Britain there was a letter waiting for him inviting him to return. A £500 purse was a big sweetener and Jack set sail for South Africa again, on the *Caledonian Castle*, and fought Williams on Christmas Eve. This time Palmer withstood the South African heavyweight challenge and was out boxing him when the heavier man lost his temper. Jack was seized round the waist and tossed out of the ring, earning Williams an instant disqualification for throwing his English opponent. A rubber match was settled on only for Jack to catch enteric fever and, after a period in hospital, he returned home.

The National Sporting Club was now supervising all official British title fights and they matched Jack with Jeffrey Thorne (real name Townsend: the ABA heavyweight champion in 1898 and 1899) for the British title. After turning professional, Thorne had toured America for a couple of years looking for lucrative fights (he lost to Bob Fitzsimmons in one round and to Kid McCoy in three). He had not boxed until recently when he had beaten an American, Charlie St Clair from Brooklyn, in one round at the National Sporting Club.

His last fight, and the fight that clinched his matching with Jack Palmer, was a six-round win over Ben Taylor. The much-vaunted pairing fought for the new title, in December 1905, over what was scheduled to be twenty rounds. However, the £350 purse was in Palmer's corner inside of four rounds. Palmer's punching troubled Thorne from the second round. Although he held his own in the following round, another sustained attack from Palmer clinched the fight in the fourth. A hard left hook, which sank into Thorne's midriff, doubled the former amateur champion in two and he was counted out not long into the round.

Unwisely Jack spent ten months out of the ring and the inactivity played its part in the Newcastle ringman losing his British title. Palmer was matched with the twenty-seven-year-old James 'Gunner' Moir from Lambeth. Moir had fought all his early contests at the London venue, Wonderland, while still serving in the Army. Moir, the heavier at around 13 stone, soon had the champion gasping with fierce body shots. With Palmer finding it hard to get into the fight in the opening rounds, Moir continually stopped him in his tracks with full-blooded swings; an early ending was seemingly obvious. In the fourth round Palmer, moving around more, started to come back into the match. He had Moir in trouble, but when he closed in to apply further pressure, Gunner's desperate swings managed to keep him at bay. By the ninth it was fairly even. Moir launched another attack, which saw Palmer reeling. He fell, but on the way down grabbed hold of his opponent to save himself. He continued to hold and foolishly hit his man whilst still in the same position. Referee J.H. Douglas called a halt and gave the title to 'Gunner' Moir on a disqualification. Moir, who would take part in the first world heavyweight title fight to take place in London, against visiting Canadian world champion Tommy Burns, later lost his British title in round one to 'Iron' Hague in 1909. By becoming the first man to beat 'Bombardier' Billy Wells, he also had an unsuccessful shot at Wells, in 1913, in his post of new champion.

Returning home he completed a two-round win at the Circus over Young John Sullivan. Shortly afterwards another fight offer arrived in the post for Jack Palmer. The letter was from the handlers of Jack 'Twin' Sullivan, explaining that there was good money available for a return match between the pair. On their way over to the west coast of America, Jack and his manager Jimmy Lowes called in at Philadelphia to try to tempt 'Philadelphia' Jack O'Brien into the ring. During his lengthy sojourn in England, O'Brien had stayed in Newcastle and a match would have been on until O'Brien's decision to return to the United States ended the plans. Since then O'Brien had beaten Bob Fitzsimmons to become world light-heavyweight champion. But the new weight division did not really interest him; he preferred to fight heavyweights. He had drawn with the new world champion, Tommy Burns. O'Brien had a return with Burns pencilled in (which he subsequently lost) at the time of Palmer's American visit and 'Philadelphia' Jack was forced to decline the fight.

Jack 'Twin' Sullivan, who would become a world title claimant himself and whose career would extend into the twenties, had become a better fighter since his first meeting with Palmer. The man who had beaten Tommy Burns before he was champion back in 1905, and drawn with O'Brien and Stanley Ketchel, knocked him down in ten rounds. Poor Jimmy Lowes was forced to throw in the towel to save Jack from being knocked senseless. Back in England, Palmer put feelers out for a return with Moir. There was a possibility of that pair meeting if the Newcastle fighting man gave a good showing in his next test.

If Jack Johnson, the outstanding challenger, had been given his world heavyweight title chance in 1906, the world would not have heard about the Canadian, Tommy Burns. Johnson did not get his fight against Marvin Hart, but the 5ft 7in Burns did, and became the lightest and smallest man to win the richest prize in sport. Tommy Burns never had a manager. The shrewd Canadian cut out the middleman and did all his own deals and, once established, never threw a punch until he got the money in his hand in advance.

Tommy arrived in London in the summer of 1907 and the National Sporting Club soon agreed to match him with the British champion, 'Gunner' Moir, for Tommy's world title. There was no doubt in Tommy's mind: unnoticed, he had observed Moir boxing in a benefit match and had learned enough to feel confident of putting a £500 bet on himself to beat the British champion. Tommy was soon up to his old tricks and the fight did not get away to 10p.m. because the unscrupulous champion refused to budge until he had £2,300 in his hand. Moir had difficulty with Burns' small frame, and especially with Tommy fighting in a crouching style. It seemed as if Burns could have won at any given time in the fight. The fighting became very one-sided before it terminated in round ten. Tommy wanted to stay on and milk the situation by staging another fight. Palmer, however, on the back of this defeat, became the fall guy when a fight was put on at Wonderland

Tommy Burns never missed a trick and he proposed to Wonderland promoter Jack Wolfe that he would fight Jack Palmer at his club. Wolfe could not relate to what extraordinary lengths Burns would go to make sure he received everything for which he had contracted. On the morning of the fight, Burns arrived with a set of new padlocks and secured all the entrances and exits, leaving only the main door as an entrance. He then set himself up in the box office and checked off the takings. He did not go to his dressing room until the house was full and he tallied all the takings. Four inches taller, but a few pounds lighter, Palmer had trained hard with sparring partners Bob Ryan and Tom Lancaster for his big chance.

After the Moir performance, the fight was predictable. Poor Jack was down nine times in three and half rounds of action. It was one of the easiest victories of Tommy Burns' career. Palmer appeared stage struck and repeatedly left himself an open target for the world champion. Occasionally Jack would let fly after a lengthened period of defence, but his efforts lacked sting and only caused Burns to smile. He was down three times in round one (counts of three, nine and eight seconds) from smarting right handers and, with little resistance, he was down for a nine count in round two and two nine counts and an eight count in round three. In the last round, he was down a further two times before being counted out. His defeat was greeted by hissing all around the club.

The month after his win over Palmer, Tommy was in Ireland for a St Patrick's day date with the Wexford blacksmith, Jem Roche. Odds were ridiculously in favour of Tommy, but with the Irish keen to show loyalty and back their own man regardless of how much of a chance he had, the odds were considerably shortened. Tommy made a bet that he would leave his hotel, win the fight, and be back in his room within half an hour. Unbelievably he managed the feat. Poor Roche was defeated in just 65 seconds, a record in the heavyweight division that remained unbeaten until 1982, in the Mike Dokes versus Mike Weaver fight. Tommy stopped over in Paris for some more easy bouts, before arriving in Australia, where Jack Johnson eventually caught up with him and took his title.

Jack retired after the comprehensive defeat by Burns but, within a year, was persuaded to return, drawing with American Bart Connolly at Birkenhead Drill Hall. The lighter American took a fearful pounding to earn a draw. There were a couple of other low key appearances heading towards the First World War and, like many who followed, Palmer was always available to give a hand to some of the later hopefuls in the North East.

Spike Robson

Very few are the British boxers who have cracked America. Bob Fitzsimmons, Owen Moran, Freddie Welsh and, after the First World War, Ted 'Kid' Lewis come readily to mind and to that celebrated list can be added Frank 'Spike' Robson. The 'no-decision' contest rule, which prevailed at the time on the American East Coast, robbed the North-Easterner of a serious attempt at a world title. One of the sport's great tacticians, he took part in two of the best remembered fights of the era between Northern fighters, in his clashes with Teessider, Johnny Summers. Later, in the twilight of his career, Robson returned from an idle spell in America to challenge Welsh legend 'Peerless' Jim Driscoll twice.

He was born in South Shields on 5 November 1877 and by the time he was in his teens he was producing his own fireworks. Publican Jimmy Lowes is reputed to be the man who gave him his first paid booking in Newcastle. Lowes paired him, over three rounds, with Bob Gullen in the room above his pub in Percy Street. Earning a couple of bob for a points win, most of young Robson's early performances were at Percy Cottage. Still only fifteen years of age, his prominence in the area was good enough to earn him work with the various boxing booths touring throughout the North. It was in the booths that Spike Robson developed his punching skills. His ability to defeat a man in quick time pushed his name forward as a fighter with a reputation to be feared.

Prize-fighting with bare fists still had not died and, if the opportunity arose for a money match with the 'raw 'uns', Spike could never resist a challenge. These illegal confrontations in secret locations always attracted the betting fraternity and on one occasion on the sand dunes at Marsden Rock Island, Frank beat Jack Thompson in forty-three rounds. Spike described those knuckle fights, which often took place on wasteland adjoining disused coal pits, thus: 'We fought anyhow and everyhow, but I thereby got to realise that the man who is going to win fights, either inside or outside a ring is the man who has brains to plan his own tactics and a few more to spare, which will enable him to adopt his talents to circumstances.'

His first recorded fight win was in 1896, when he scored a knockout win over Will Corbett in thirteen rounds. There was no short route to the championship in this era and Spike campaigned mostly in the north, particularly in Newcastle where he had his own popularity, and was a guaranteed seat-filler in the Geordie heartland. His two fights with Pedlar Palmer (world and British bantamweight champion from 1895 to 1899 – Spike drew and lost on points in these bouts), and three with George Dixon (who had claimed both bantamweight and featherweight world titles – Spike won twice) helped promote the South Shields fighter on the international stage.

Spike made a claim to the British featherweight title (fixed at 9 stone in 1901) when he beat Jack Roberts. At the National Sporting Club in 1904, Roberts took part in one of boxing's most important court cases, when the legality of boxing was under examination after the death of Murray Livingstone, who boxed under the name of Billy Smith in 1901. Smith had died after falling and striking his head during a contest with Roberts at the National Sporting Club. Roberts, along with nine of the leading members of the club, were committed to the Old Bailey and charged with 'feloniously killing and slaying Livingstone'. The trial was a test case; the lead counsel for the prosecution stated that the case was being brought as an effort to stop boxing rather than to exact punishment on the accused. The jury's verdict in the case was one of accidental death; while they appreciated there was an inseparable risk in boxing, the contest had taken place under proper rules and the accused were not guilty. The official champion, Ben Jordan, had been campaigning in America. Champion since 1899, on his return he defeated Pedlar Palmer, but, during 1905, Jordan retired. British bantamweight champion, Joe Bowker, then made his claim after beating Palmer, but the match was made at 8 stone 12 pounds even though it was declared to be for the championship. In January of the following year, the Sporting Club gave blessing to a 9 stone match between Spike Robson and Johnny Summers for the British featherweight title. Three months before he met Johnny, Spike had lost a twenty-round decision to Joe Bowker. Robson's right to challenge for the now officially endorsed title raised questions, but in fact it is questionable whether Bowker had the right to call himself British featherweight champion anyway. Johnny Summers had the better of the twenty-round contest between the two North-East fighters. After the fight, Spike did what a lot of top British boxers of the time were electing to do: he caught a boat to try his luck in America.

Making his home in Philadelphia, Spike was engaged in eight no-decision six-rounders. The impressive run ended in a visit to New York where Billy Ryan stopped him over nine rounds. When news filtered through of a title return with his old rival Summers, planned by the National Sporting Club, Robson returned to London. For four rounds the well-matched pair threw everything at each other until, during a fierce rally, Spike was pushed into the ropes and, becoming entangled, he slipped to the floor. Johnny could not resist throwing several blows and the referee disqualified him and gave the title to Robson. Johnny moved up into the lightweight ranks after the fight and Spike Robson returned across the water with the extra clout of being able to call himself British featherweight champion.

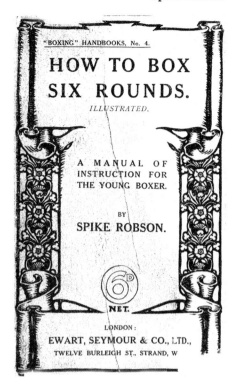

Spike Robson, the South Shields boxer who took on the best in America.

Spike's book, which includes accounts of his famous fights in America.

Settling back in Philadelphia, approaching thirty, and at the peak of his career with half a life's experience in the ring, Spike raised the pedigree of British boxing even higher with a string of great displays against the best men in the States. Boxing in this period in America was mostly limited to six-round, no-decision bouts. That meant that, even in title fights, no boxer could win a fight unless he did so by knockout. It also meant that champions were safe as long as hard-punching opponents were avoided when putting titles at stake. During this period of no-decision bouts, newspaper reporters gave their own verdicts, though they did not carry enough weight to deprive a champion of his title. The situation was relevant to New York State and no-decision bouts were not phased out until the introduction of the Walker Law in 1920.

Young Frank Erne was the hero of Philadelphia and was considered unbeatable at his weight. However, despite giving away six pounds, Spike was keen for a match. (Erne won the world lightweight title in 1898, then slimmed down to challenge Terry McGovern for the featherweight title, but was taken out in three rounds. The only Swiss-born fighter to win a world title, he made an unsuccessful bid for the welterweight title, but was stopped in nine rounds by Rube Ferns and, in 1902, he lost his lightweight title to Joe Gans.) Public opinion thought

Erne would wear Robson down and stop him inside six rounds. Erne brimmed with confidence from the start, but soon started to suffer as Spike's jabs and body blows made their marks. Erne was too experienced to back off. In the fourth round, Spike noticed his body punches starting to slide off. The American's seconds had oiled their man between rounds. Robson moved upstairs and at the end of six rounds he had made quite a mess of Frank's face.

Soon after his fight with Erne, Robson was matched against another giant of the American ring, Abe Attell. When only seventeen, in 1901, the Jewish-American had claimed the world featherweight title after out-pointing George Dixon. Terry McGovern was the official champion and it wasn't until 1904 that Abe was able to strengthen his claim by beating Harry Forbes. By then McGovern had lost his crown to Corbett who then relinquished it following weight problems. A story exists that Spike Robson pared his nails down to the quick in order to make the stipulated 124 pounds weight limit. Despite being younger in years than Spike, Attell had a shrewd boxing brain. A terrific hitter, Abe could also box defensively and Spike, suspecting Attell would rattle up the points by keeping away from him, decided to attack the jaw from the first bell. Attell was convinced that Robson would slog it to the end and became confused when the Englishman changed tactics after throwing some heavy punches. Robson, breaking away, gave an exhibition of his dancing footwork before coming back to the fray. Having laid his plan for a slogging match and expecting to pick Robson off, Abe was unsure whether Spike was bluffing. After three rounds, Attell knew he was being out-pointed and had become visibly upset. Knowing he had to make up the leeway, he waded into fight at the start of the fifth round. This is what Robson was waiting for, because he knew he was in with a chance in a fight game rather than a six-rounder where Attell could decide his tactics and pull the strings. Abe cut loose but, although he had a great reputation as a hitter, he could not match the punching power of Spike Robson. Attell knew he had been beaten in the no-decision bout and the fight spoiled Robson's chances of a world title fight. Promoters were interested in the pairing, but Attell insisted on a fight being fixed at 8 stone 10 pounds. Spike could not make the weight. If he dieted heavily, he might have taken the fight at 8 stone 12 pounds, but even that would have meant a starve and sweat session, which he felt was too big a gamble.

Known as the 'Old Master', the American Negro Joe Gans was the first great thinking man's fighter. Gans was a boxer who could feint, slip a punch and counter without taking more than half a step. Until Benny Leonard appeared on the scene in the following decade, Gans was regarded as the greatest lightweight in history. He was foiled in his first attempt at a world title when Frank Erne stopped him in twelve rounds (Gans was ahead on points and was severely criticised for quitting with a cut eye). Fully prepared for the return, Gans knocked out Erne in the first round to take his title. It was alleged that Joe threw a fight with Terry McGovern after a two-round knockout, but after that Gans was only beaten once in the subsequent eight years. That was when he conceded weight to Sam Langford and went fifteen rounds. Often fighting in the higher weight divisions, Gans fought a twenty-round draw with Joe Walcott in a bid to win the world welterweight title in 1904. In September 1906, Joe fought an epic contest with 'Battling' Nelson in Nevada. The fight, scheduled for forty-five rounds, had gone forty-two, before Nelson was disqualified for throwing a low punch.

Spike got his chance with the 'Old Master' in Philadelphia in 1908 and the pairing was a big draw. Robson wisely got twice as much as Gans for the fight because he insisted on a percentage of the gate receipts while Joe took a lump sum. Spike ran into a bit of bad luck, for had he been successful in going the distance with a boxer of the stature of Gans, he would have gained several months work in vaudeville and could have secured his own price for short fights in a number of towns. An accident in training for the world lightweight title fight (the fight was a no-decision, but Gans' title was at risk if he lost inside the distance) cost Robson an estimated £10,000 to £20,000. The North-Easterner had slipped on a pebble while running and had wrenched his knee. On reflection afterwards he stated that he should have called the fight off. The reason he did not was because a £200 slice of his money had been guaranteed on his appearance. Bandaging up the knee, he hoped for the best, thinking he would be too quick on his feet for Gans to catch him, even at long range. Convinced he could not lose the six-round fight, Robson knew the 'Old Master' would be at his most dangerous on the break, where his speciality short hooks came into play. Getting in and out quickly, Robson was having the better of the first three rounds, until Gans rushed him onto the ropes and, with a right cross, buckled Robson's knees. Spike rolled out of the ring in pain and, when it was obvious he could hardly stand, the referee refused to let him continue. Joe Gans was still champion, but later in the year he lost his title in the return with 'Battling' Nelson. Seventeen months later, at the age of thirty-five, the great champion was dead of consumption, brought on, it was surmised, by starving himself to lose weight for fights.

Other notables Robson fought during his American period were Johnny Dwyer, Kid Stringer, Frank Carsey, Al Grander and Jack Daley. Spike boxed Grover Hayes twice in no-decision bouts and held his own against 'Terrible' Terry McGovern and 'Harlem' Tommy Murphy. 'Battling' Nelson (nicknamed the 'Durable Dane') was reputed to be the toughest man ever seen in a ring. In well over a hundred fights he was only stopped twice. One of the men to beat him was English featherweight Owen Moran. But neither Owen nor Nelson wanted to meet Spike Robson in spite of the fact that, in Nelson's case, Spike offered £1,000 of his own money.

Spike had returned to England on one or two trips and, in 1910, having reached his early thirties, decided that he wanted to finish his career back in England. His arrival coincided with Jim Driscoll's six-round stoppage win over 'Seaman' Arthur Hayes at the National Sporting Club. Jim was a claimant of the British featherweight title, having beaten Joe Bowker twice, and the Sporting Club gave official backing for a fight between Driscoll and Hayes for the first Lonsdale Belt awarded in the featherweight division. Spike duly arrived at the famous club to put forward his challenge to the newly crowned champion. His challenge could not be ignored. He argued, 'How can there be a new featherweight champion of England when the old one is alive and kicking?' Spike had a point but, although he had been out of the country, he had not defended the British title he had won in 1906. There was no problem with Driscoll: he accepted the challenge immediately. The decision was left with the club promoter 'Peggy' Bettinson. The promoter had always rated Robson, who had proved his credibility with his performances in America and Bettinson was proud to announce the fight could be held in two months time. Robson immediately pulled out a fist of £5 notes, deposited his side stake, and confessed to the club members that he had not fought for twenty-one months but had kept fit in the gym.

Carrying an upright fighting position, with conspicuous use of the left lead, Jim Driscoll, widely known as 'Old Peerless', was often portrayed as the perfect exponent of the 'English Style'. Irish by extraction, Welsh by birth, Jim had learned and adopted his own style of boxing. Coming through boys' competitions and then the booths, Jim, whose ring science was thought to be unrivalled, loved fighting for fighting's sake. He also had a reputation as one of the cleanest boxers going. With Jim there was little clinching and no blindside tricks out of the way of the referee. Driscoll had also tasted American success, fighting many of the men with whom Spike had got in the ring in the United States. A year earlier he had gone ten rounds with Abe Attell in New York in a world title challenge. The no-decision fight enabled Attell to stay champion. Confidence was never in short supply from Spike as he quoted in his book: 'I was as sure of winning the first battle, as I have ever been certain about anything. I knew Jim – I'd studied him for years – and I knew he was a better boxer than I was, quite possibly the best in the world.' So sure was Spike of winning that he laid a lot of money on himself and got good odds. The betting was 5-1 against Spike. Robson laid his plan. His tactics were based on the fact that he was so sure Driscoll and his friends thought they had an easy task on their hands that he meant to let Jim think it was an easier job that he had imagined. The National Sporting Club members were shocked when Robson entered the ring, for, in contrast to Jim's black curly hair, Spike had shaved his head. The club members had gone for Driscoll primarily because Robson, at four years older, had been fightless for two years. After the first three rounds, the odds had gone up 10-1 against Spike. The older man's tactics not only shocked the onlookers outside the ring, but they knocked the Welshman completely out of his stride. Spike was all over the ring, ducking and diving but not really trading punches. Jim tried to catch Spike as he came in. Most of the time Spike was moving around, but some punches did land and although he was not happy, Driscoll did start to take a points lead.

Robson landed his first real punch in round four, when a short left closed Driscoll's left eye. Robson had feinted a right swing and then thrown a one-two with his left. It was obvious the Welshman was in trouble and, to some degree, the bell saved him from further punishment. The odds had now dropped back to evens. As the gong sounded for round five, Spike bounded out of his corner brimming with confidence. His plan was to catch Driscoll unaware and snare him in the corner. At the last second, Driscoll coolly side-stepped and the Welshman's split second timing saw Robson stub his toe and slip onto the chair that Driscoll's second was taking out of the ring. The skin of his shaven head was cut open and blood poured down his face. Still dazed he beckoned Driscoll to continue fighting and, after a second or two of shocked reluctance, Driscoll rejoined his rival.

Robson would have been better retiring then, because the fight was to go another ten rounds, about which Spike was to remember nothing. Robson's courage impressed the club members, but the incident had seen the tide turn. For several rounds, Robson appeared like a drunken man, holding on or leaning on his man in the clinch. Boxing at long range, Driscoll demonstrated his artistry, producing six lighting jabs without return. Spike still appeared game, but as the fight went on, Driscoll seemed able to do what he wanted with impunity. As the fight became more and more one-sided, Driscoll knew the only way his opponent would surrender was by him administering a knockout blow. That eventuality came in round fifteen. Forcing Spike into a corner, the Welshman caught him full on the mouth with a vicious left. The punch had left Robson unguarded and Driscoll followed up with a right smash to the jaw. Spike fell halfway through the ropes and the fight was over. No one in the club could believe their eyes when Robson rose at the count of three. Driscoll fed him another right. Spike went down again and amazingly rose at six, but, before Jim could throw another punch, Robson had fallen backwards hitting the boards with a bang. Robson was unconscious for a long time and reportedly did not wake fully for four days. The club committee and doctors were scared, for there was a belief that Robson had made a close call on his own life and they were unwilling to give the former champion a return encounter.

Driscoll returned to America, but returned for a bitter fight with his rival, Freddie Welsh. The two men detested each other. Freddie had done nearly all his fighting in America and was schooled in stateside roughhouse tactics. The clash was reputed to be the only time 'Old Peerless' ever fought dirty. Late in the fight he abandoned all his trademark styles and became a street fighter for a night. Welsh got the decision on a disqualification. Police had to break up fights in the Rink stadium, including a grapple between rival seconds who were giving good impressions of their respective champions.

Five weeks later, Driscoll met Spike with an outright Lonsdale Belt the target for the stylish Welshman. Robson had argued that the chair incident had lost him the first fight. There was plenty of support for him in his belief. He even hinted that it had been a smart move by Driscoll's second in catching him so neatly with the chair whilst carrying it out of the ring. The return took place nine months after their first meeting and, anticipating another incident-fuelled fight, the Sporting Club was designated as standing room only. Driscoll was again the favourite, but this time the starting odds were slight. Jim looked in perfect condition and, as he had boxed Robson before, those in the know backed Driscoll. Despite his experience, Driscoll was a learner, and if a man did beat him (he only lost three out of seventy-one professional fights), there was no way it would happen again. Though punching lighter than his opponent, Jim showed amazing speed and accuracy. Robson played it cagey, preferring to keep on the move and let Driscoll do the leading.

For a while it turned into an exhibition bout rather than a championship contest. Spike then lost interest in his negative approach and switched tactics. Driscoll was ready and Spike was meeting a man who, at his weight at this moment in time, was the best in the world. As Spike tried to rush and swing, Driscoll coolly picked him off with a display of brilliant counter-punching which had the Sporting Club members off their seats. Remembering the punishment Spike had taken in the first encounter, the referee was not prepared to let the fight continue until he collapsed. In the sixth round, he left his chair outside the ring in order to get a closer view of the damage Driscoll's punching was doing. Spike was weakening and a left hook to the chin felled him. Not wanting to lose face, Robson was up by only two in the referee's count. The left jabbing into Spike's face like a machine gun just wore the South Shields man away and, by the seventh round, the fight was beginning to become one-way traffic, a fact that made the referee bring proceedings to halt. Switching his plan to the puncher's chance had been the wrong tactics against a world-class champion. Clearly upset with the referee's decision, Spike admitted he had gone through a rough passage, but added that he thought Driscoll's punches had lost their sting and that Jim was starting to weaken near the end. Spike got the club doctor to examine him and give a statement, to no avail, that Spike was still fit and strong. Spike had planned both his fights with Driscoll and felt that, without the part ill luck had played, he certainly would have won one, if not both, of his tussles with the Welshman.

After that second defeat, Spike retired and concentrated on running a boxing academy, passing on his knowledge to aspiring youngsters. In 1915, he returned to the ring and boxed an eight-round draw with Joe Skinner, but realised a serious comeback was beyond him. Spike settled down to live in Harehills near Leeds and died, in his eightieth year, at his daughter's house at Rotherham in 1957. In 1925 the pavements of Cardiff were lined with 100,000 mourners paying tribute to Spike's conqueror, Tim Driscoll. The procession, nearly a mile long and featuring many great fighters, paid their final respects to one of the all-time greats of the sport, who died of consumption in his early forties.

Johnny Summers

In line with the boxing boom that was sweeping the country in the seven or eight years prior to the First World War, British boxing, particularly in the middle-weight ranges (featherweight to welterweight), was at its strongest. The North East could boast Jim Driscoll, Freddie Welsh, Johnny Basham, Gerry Delaney, Boy McCormick and Spike Robson, while doing Yorkshire proud in that celebrated company, was Middlesbrough-born, Johnny Summers. In a six-year period, from 1906 to 1912, Summers lay claim to British titles at feather, light and welterweight and, like many of his contemporaries of the era, successfully toured in both America and Australia.

Born in 1883, Johnny left his native North East as a youngster and was brought up in Canning Town. Never boxing as an amateur – not many could afford to in those days – his career started at seventeen and, before it was over twenty years later, the square-jawed, fair-headed Yorkshireman would amass 179 fights, sixteen of which were title fights, claiming 104 wins, 29 draws and 14 no-decision contests.

Jimmy Butler, the father of Frank, the famous newspaper journalist, labelled Summers, who was an expert at strength-hitting, the hardest punching lightweight he ever saw. 'Old Jimmy', who ran his own boxing booth road show for years, had seen a few in his time. Both the leading referees of the era were full of praise for Johnny. Eugene Corri in his 1919 book *Reminiscences of Boxing* called him 'the quickest little fighting gentleman in the world', adding 'he talks very little, but is a most excellent listener'. Charlie Rose, in a later publication, *Life's a Knockout*, christened Johnny, 'the mildest mannered fighter he had ever met', although Rose warned it was a different story when he had the gloves on.

Summers, who was actually born Johnny Somers, was a devout Roman Catholic and freely gave his earnings from the ring to a local church. Before and after every round he crossed himself. Another idiosyncrasy of the man was to enter the ring with a rosary tucked down his socks, which he could touch for luck when the opportunity arose. Sometimes his corner carried a crucifix and, although the practice of taking his religion to work caused many jibes, Johnny took them all in good part. Jimmy Britt, whom Summers met in several contests said afterwards, tongue firmly planted in his cheek: 'The only thing I didn't like about the contest was that habit of making the sign of the cross, at the commencement of every round, appealing to the almighty to give a guy like me a hiding. I don't think he was very fond of him, because Summers never hurt me.'

Johnny acknowledged the devoutness did him good and helped with his work: 'Fighting is my profession and I am not ashamed of it. If I introduced my religion into my daily occupation, it is no more than any good Catholic ought to do. Some people look down on boxing as coarse and brutalising. I call it manly and no way demoralising.'

In his first year in the sport (1900), as an eighteen-year-old, Johnny had eight contests, winning five and drawing two. His first defeat came from the hands of Tibby Watson. Over the next few years an array of impressive names started to appear on his victory list. He beat George Corfield and Fred Delaney and, in three clashes with Cockney Cohen in 1903, he won, lost on points and drew the other. Boxing as a featherweight (the weight had become world standardised at 9 stone in 1900), Johnny had a London rival, in the shape of Young Joseph, who was two years Johnny's junior. Joseph hailed from Aldgate, the birth place of another boxing Jew, Ted 'Kid' Lewis. Born Aschel Joseph, the London youngster met Johnny six times between 1904 and 1907 with honours even (two points-wins each and two draws). In their later fights, Johnny beat him twice in 1912, knocking him out on one occasion and winning a twenty-round points decision for the British welterweight title in their other confrontation.

A draw with the British featherweight champion from two years earlier, Jack Roberts, put Johnny into the championship frame. British title fights in the early days of the century were before the inception of the National Sporting Club and Lonsdale Belts. There was often difficulty in clarifying champions with titles frequently having more than one claimant. Fellow North-Easterner Spike Robson had laid claim to the 9 stone championships by defeating Jack Roberts in a title fight in 1904 at Drury Lane. Another claimant was the Lancastrian, Joe Bowker, who had been British bantamweight champion for three years. Bowker's 1905 victory over Pedlar Palmer, who hailed from Johnny's neighbourhood of Canning Town, was hailed as one the sport's greatest contests. The affair ended when Palmer, who claimed the world bantamweight title in 1895 but did not manage to get American recognition, failed to come out for the thirteenth round. Bowker subsequently defeated Robson, but instead of fighting Bowker, who was still British bantam champion, Johnny was matched with Robson, for the British featherweight title, three months after Robson had lost to Bowker. Johnny laid his claim by beating Robson over twenty rounds. But, before 1906 was out, he had lost a return match to Robson when he was disqualified for punching Spike when he was down. Before losing his title, Johnny had defended successfully against 'Seaman' Arthur Hayes and 'Boss' Edwards.

Johnny Summers, the hard-punching Yorkshire lightweight who became British and British Empire welterweight champion.

The following year, Johnny toured America, sharing no-decision contests with the likes of 'Harlem' Tommy Murphy and Young Erne in Philadelphia and Bert Keyes who he fought four times on his return to New York in 1908.

When he fought in England again, Summers campaigned as a lightweight and was soon in title action at his new weight. Jack Goldswain had been British lightweight champion since 1906, but once again there was controversy as to whether Goldswain was the correct champion. Bermondsey boy Goldswain had caused a surprise by out-pointing Jabez White over twenty rounds at the National Sporting Club in April 1906. The match with White had been made at 10 stone (140 pounds), but it was billed as being for the British lightweight championship. White refused to relinquish the crown claiming he had been beaten in an overweight bout, because the lightweight limit was at 9 stone 9 pounds. Confusion raged, though Goldswain did receive acknowledgement of a decision made by the editor of *Mirror of Life*, who declared him champion. Goldswain had only started boxing when he lost some of his fingers in a tin can factory and was subsequently sacked for being unable to do the job. He had boxed on the Summers *v.* Robson bill at the National Sporting Club, but had been inactive in recent weeks preferring to work the music hall circuit. His inactivity had seen the pounds pile on and rumours put his weight as high as 11 stone 7 pounds. Goldswain still wanted the fight and came to the scale at 10 stone 4 pounds, losing something like 16 pounds in seven days. After nine rounds, Johnny had boxed him to a standstill. Goldswain was down once in the tenth and three times in the fourteenth, at which point the referee raised Johnny's hand as champion. Goldswain moved up to welterweight: a route the new champion would also take in the not too distant future.

Prior to the Goldswain fight, Johnny had lost a highly disputed points decision to Jimmy Britt at the London venue, Wonderland. Summers was very keen to avenge the result against the great little scrapper from San Francisco, who had been in the ring with all the great American lightweights like Battling Nelson, Joe Gans and Packy McParland. Johnny beat Britt over twenty rounds in the return at the National Sporting Club and, with the needle between the two boxers so great, there was obvious interest in a third fight. In the rubber match at the Memorial Grounds in West Ham, Summers started to get on top and, by the ninth round, the crowd started to get excited as the American looked to be exhausted in the heat. Britt sank to one knee and Billy Tucker, who claimed to be the world champion ball puncher, rushed from the corner to shower Britt with a soaked sponge. Summers, outraged by Tucker's entry, leapt to remonstrate but was held back by the referee. At this stage the crowd stampeded. The result was that fighting broke out and spectators seeking safety had no alternative but to climb into the ring. An organised gang, estimated by Jimmy Butler to be over 200 strong, took command of the situation and, with lightning speed, stripped spectators of their wallets. The gang was particularly severe on a party of rich Americans who were relieved of watches and diamonds in the mêlée. For a long time afterwards, open-air promotions were badly attended, When Britt and Summers called for their fight money, the cashier had already departed. Johnny eventually cornered one of the partners in the promotion and, with backing from some local tough customers, he refused to leave until he was received some remuneration. Reportedly, all Britt was paid was £75. Needless to say the American, who was an expert on Shakespeare's works, never fought in London again

Freddie Welsh had upheld Britain's traditions in the American ring and the Welshman had now returned home to Britain. Supremely confident, though sometimes his bombastic attitude cost him many friends, Welsh was not only a great defensive ringman, but he could in-fight with the best. He has often been described as one of our greatest-ever lightweights. His career was from 1908–22; in 168 fights he tasted only four defeats, though through his long American campaigns eighty-one of his fights were no-decision. When the National Sporting Club presented their first Lonsdale Belt for the lightweight division, Johnny was invited to meet Welsh in November 1908. Ten weeks before the fight, Welsh had retired Henri Piet to win the European title at Mountain Ash. The European title was not at stake – only Johnny's British title – and Welsh was convincing enough to take the honours over twenty rounds. While Johnny's next entrance in the championship arena would be at welterweight, Welsh lost his title in his first defence against Matt Wells. Regaining his title in a return with Wells, Freddie held the British lightweight title from 1912 to 1919, although he hardly defended it, preferring to spend time in America in a more lucrative market. He won the world title off Willie Richie in 1917 and, after two no-decision bouts against Benny Leonard, the American beat him at the third attempt in 1919, becoming the only man to knock Welsh out. Retiring in 1922, Welsh died five years later at the age of forty-one.

Moving up to welterweight, Summers spent most of 1910 fighting in Australia, remaining unbeaten during his tour. The next championship fight came in January of 1911 and Johnny, for the first of only two occasions in his career, contested a version of the world title. Since the eclipse of Joe Walcott in 1906, several claimants had contested the world welterweight championship. Irish-American Honey Mellody claimed the title, having beaten Walcott, and pre-1910 other American claimants included Joe Thomas, Mike 'Twin' Sullivan, Jimmy Gardner, Jack Blackburn and Harry Lewis. The aggressive style of the Jewish-American Lewis was well known in the country and had seen off the best fighters Britain could throw at him. Harry claimed the championship when he beat Mellody in April of 1908. Only 'Private' Palmer and Johnny Mathieson were able to get decisions over him in his many fights in the country. The American was particularly popular at Wonderland, where he often entered the ring smoking a cigar, a trademark imitated by another American who tangled with Johnny – Harry Stone. 'Private' Harris, 'Seaman' Hull, Jimmy Horman and Jack Harrison were all stopped inside the distance at the famous London venue. Johnny's rival, Young Joseph, got his world title chance with Lewis, but could not survive past seven rounds. When Johnny's chance with Lewis came six months later, he failed to handle the world champion's punching power and, for the first time in his career, he failed to beat the count and lasted only four rounds. Lewis elected to move up to middleweight.

Later in the year, Summers was knocked out for the second time by a top fighter from across the Atlantic. The victor was another American who preferred to box in Europe. The 'Dixie Kid' was an American Negro with a real name of Aaron L. Brown. At his best the 'Kid' weighed under 10 stone, but was willing to fight anyone from welterweight to heavyweight. In April 1904, he had beaten the West Indian, Joe Walcott, on a foul and had also drawn in a second fight with the champion. 'Dixie Kid' had every right to be recognised as a champion, but the claim was not followed through and the 'Kid' elected to try his luck in England. 'Dixie' insisted on arrival that he was twenty-seven years old, but others who knew him understood him to be nearer to forty. A clever but clumsy looking fighter, 'Dixie' often lost fights on purpose. He contended that if he did not drop a decision every now and then he would fail to get enough fights to pay the rent. He was a master of buffoonery, with timing so good that he often boxed with one hand anchored on the ropes. Later deported, he turned up boxing in Germany, eventually returning to America where he died in poverty. Johnny lost to 'Dixie' at that graveyard of champions – Liverpool (the promoters at the stadium, who were known never to miss a trick, billed the fight as for the world title at 142 pounds). Unbeatable against his own countrymen, it was a surprise when the 'Kid' knocked him out in only two rounds.

In April 1912, Johnny met his old rival, Young Joseph, for a fight billed as a decider for the British welterweight title. Since moving to welterweight, Joseph had won the first Lonsdale Belt offered in the division and after beating Jack Goldswain on a disqualification in 1910, the Jewish fighter was champion for a second time. Joseph claimed the European title when he beat the Frenchman, 'Battling' Lacroix, but then lost his titles to Kent fighter, Arthur Evernden, in a third-round disqualification. Evernden claimed the European title, but the title was not recognised as his on the rest of the continent. Joseph continued to be accepted as European champion and beat Robert Eustache over fifteen rounds in Paris. Joseph lost his title to Georges Carpentier whom 'old Dixie' had given a few lessons to earlier. Because Joseph had put his British title on the line when meeting Evernden, his meeting with Johnny was generally not accepted as a championship contest. Johnny had the better of Joseph over twenty rounds and, to confirm his supremacy over Joseph, he knocked him out in the same year, becoming the first man to do so.

Arthur Evernden could not claim the British welterweight title until he had disposed of Joseph's conqueror. Evernden's speciality weapon was a left hand of explosive quality and not everyone was convinced that Johnny would beat him. The action boiled over as early as round three when both fighters hooked simultaneously: Arthur went down while Johnny struggled to stay on his feet. Both men recovered and the fight came to a conclusion in round thirteen. Summers stopped the Kent man to confirm (the Lonsdale Belt was issued) his welterweight championship. After a successful defence against Sid Burns, Johnny returned to Australia for the next three years, 1912 to 1914.

Burns, who had fought Summers twice, with one result each, was Johnny's first championship opponent in Sydney. Summers, now around the age of thirty, repeated his earlier twenty-round points win in a fight for the vacant British Empire title. Arthur Evernden came out to Melbourne to challenge for Johnny's new title. This time Arthur went the distance but was unable to relieve Johnny of his title.

Tom McCormick, whose ring career had only started in 1911, challenged Johnny for the Empire title (Johnny's British title was supposedly on the line too, but with the fight being in Australia official sanction was difficult). It was a big surprise when the Irishman, who had fought in less than a quarter of the number of bouts as Summers, beat him over twenty rounds in Sydney. A fortnight later the man from Dundalk took the world title off Waldemar Holberg, in a sixth-round disqualification in Melbourne. Three weeks after that, Summers and the Irishman met again, with three titles on the line (again the British leg of the title fight did not carry official recognition: the National Sporting Club neither backed the fight nor awarded a Lonsdale Belt). Johnny attacked from the opening bell, but it was McCormick who quickly took over. The action came thick and fast and poor Johnny was disposed of in only two and a half minutes. A month later it was Matt Wells, adding to the growing band of British fighters in Australia, who relieved McCormick of his titles. The Irishman, inside ten weeks, had fought four title fights, won three different titles and then lost them all.

Back in England in the second half of 1914, with the National Sporting Club not recognising Wells, Johnny, arguing that he had in fact never lost his British title, was matched with the main challenger, Johnny Basham, for the vacant title. Although there was no marked deterioration in his physical appearance, it was debated as to whether Johnny, at thirty-one, had 'many more Summers in him'. Basham, a sergeant in the Welsh Fusiliers, was seven years younger than his opponent and was made the 6-4 favourite. Johnny trained with the soldiers (it was 1914 and his old country was engaged in its own fight) at Shoeburyness, and when the press visited the camp they expressed how at home Summers felt among their company. The Yorkshireman delighted onlookers by letting the biggest soldier punch his jaw as he pleased. Johnny believed no man in England could knock him out and so did many others; the fight produced many big bets among the sporting club gentry.

Johnny needed one more win to gain his outright Lonsdale Belt. That win could have been in his grasp, but for one unguarded moment when he left himself open and encountered one of the most decisive knockout punches thrown in a ring. Basham was winning the fight; Summers was losing it through defensive errors. Eugene Corri on the other hand, whilst rating Basham as the best welterweight he had ever seen, stated he never saw Johnny Summers box better than in his fight with the Welshman. Time and again, he made Basham miss, not by inches, but by feet and. in the opinion of the majority of onlookers. Johnny should have won. Basham's recent fights had produced a run of points victories and the press had speculated as to whether he could throw a knockout punch. How wrong they proved to be. Basham was clearly in trouble in the first two rounds as Summers delighted his supporters with his famed one-two, a left hook to the midriff followed by a right to the jaw. Basham did extremely well to keep Johnny at bay, earning plaudits by escaping from tight positions. Summers brought Basham to the floor in round two as the fight odds changed in favour of the Yorkshireman. Basham had the wherewithal to realise that the close range fighting was handing the decision to his opponent, so he changed his tactics. Johnny had decided that the longer the fight went on the slimmer his chances of a points win, so he started to take chances regardless of the punishment. Johnny's cocksure attitude earned a ringside quote 'does Summers think he's immortal?' Trying to lure the challenger into close range, Johnny fell into Basham's trap. The Welshman fooled him into thinking he had punched out and, seizing one of Johnny's invitations, Basham let fly with a punch he had reserved for the right moment. Basham had ended Summers' suicidal tactics after nine rounds. Once Basham unfurled his punch, few expected Johnny ever to get up.

In the following year, Johnny Basham made his name by becoming the first boxer from the welterweight division to win an outright Lonsdale Belt. He held his title until 1920 when Ted 'Kid' Lewis knocked him out. Basham could not handle Lewis, who knocked him out in two other title fights, and stopped him later in the twenties, when the Welshman was on a comeback trail. Basham had beaten Tom McCormick in his first defence. There were no more title chances for the Irishman; he was killed during the First World War in 1916, aged twenty-six.

Johnny got his return with Basham the year after his title loss. Eugene Corri refereed the non-title bout at Liverpool Stadium. Both men were eager to prove they had learnt a lesson from the first fight. All Basham's principal fights had been held in Liverpool and the venue was packed to the rafters to witness the return. An over-cautious approach by both men restricted the early rounds. While Summers looked better at the in-fighting, Basham had come on again since the first fight and it was he who took the points decision. It had been the third time the famous referee had officiated a Summers fight and it had been the third time Johnny had lost, but there were no complaints from the former champion.

Though the fights were fewer during the war, Johnny was still working in the boxing ring and it was a surprise in 1919 when Johnny stepped back into the lightweight ranks, to meet Bermondsey boy Bob Marriott for the vacant British title. Marriott, after winning ABA titles in 1912 and 1914, had turned pro during the war, but had not yet reached double figures in his tally of fights in the paid ranks, although he had won the European title on a disqualification, after only three rounds, against Raymond Vittet.

The occasion was the sixteenth time that Johnny Summers had entered the championship arena and it would be the last. It had been seven years since Summers had fought for the lightweight crown and after nineteen years in the sport, and at thirty-six years of age, he was eleven years older than Marriott. In one of his last fights, Marriott had beaten Fred Blakeborough when the Bradford man's seconds had forced Fred to quit. The forecast was that, despite his years, Summers would have too much ring craft for the Londoner. Johnny had planned to end the action early, but Marriott's extra reach proved a problem. By the ninth round Johnny's plan had failed and it looked to ringsiders as if he had shot his bolt when he began to hang on for a points win. This earned him reprimands from the referee. Failure to heed the warnings proved costly, though, and Johnny was sent to the dressing room in round ten. Marriott collected his £450 purse and a £100 side bet, but the experience did not herald a wave of success for the new champion: within a year Marriott had retired with a remarkable record of ten fights, eight wins and British and European titles.

Johnny stepped into the ring for the last time in 1921, but, despite 179 fights in the professional arena, in 1923 they were holding benefits for the Teessider who had run into financial difficulty. Travelling had featured strongly in Johnny's life. He toured Australia as a youngster before returning home to pursue a career. He had returned again Down Under prior to the First World War and when he died in 1946 he was living in New Zealand.

Jack 'Cast Iron' Casey

His fighting name might remind one of a fifties comic character, but Jack 'Cast Iron' Casey was larger than life. Billed originally as 'Newsboy' Casey, Jack's reputation of never being knocked out in the ring in 224 fights made him the best remembered of Wearside boxers during the thirties boom when good boxers in Sunderland were prevalent.

Jack Casey was born in the Southwick area of Sunderland in 1908, before moving to the east end of the town. Educated at Gray School, Jack was an all-round sportsman, an above average swimmer and captain of the school football team. His interest in boxing developed once he had left school and visited the local boxing halls. After leaving school, young Casey worked selling papers on a street corner. As a result of attending shows promoted by the Black Brothers at Holmeside Stadium with his friends, he decided to enter a novice's flyweight competition at the stadium in 1926. It was not a spur of the moment decision because Jack had already prepared himself in training. He entered the ring wearing, what he later described in an interview as, 'old knicks and sand shoes'. Casey won that first fight in round one and boxed a draw in the final. Casey Senior, like most of the North-East fighters' fathers, had donned the gloves too and Jack was soon sparring with the rest of the young hopefuls at Duggie Morton's school of boxing. Quickly developing into a six-round boxer, by midway through 1927, the Sunderland teenager was participating in ten-rounders. With so many readymade venues wanting to incorporate Jack's aggressive style on their bills, Casey was soon appearing at South Shields, Tyne Dock, Jarrow, Hetton le Hole, Washington and Newcastle. His record for 1927 was twenty-two wins and two draws from thirty fights. In his first bout out of the area, Jack was retired by the referee at Carlisle Infantry Drill Hall. Peel Bell had the honour of being the first man to stop Jack Casey in the ring. His record the following year was three losses from twenty-eight fights and, after boxing in the Manchester area (he stayed with an uncle and boxed at Royton, Salford and Ashton under Lyme) and Leeds, Casey had broadened his reputation across the north of England. Jack told the story that he stormed off from Manchester quickly because of a row with his girlfriend. Jack never wore a collar and tie and refused to bow to his girlfriend's wishes to do so.

Harry 'Kid' Furness, well known in Manchester circles, was the first promoter to put Casey at the top of a bill. Jack got £3 for his fifteen-round encounter with local lad Al Kenny at the Adelphi Athletic Club in Salford. A famous name from pre-First World War boxing, 'Bombardier' Billy Wells, refereed the fight and his decision to award a draw did not go down well with the Salford fans who thought Casey had had much the better of the fight against their man. The fact that the crowd had booed the British boxing legend made the nationals the next day and gave young Casey his first real publicity.

The success of the first two years had guaranteed him more top-billing engagements, but his move to fight better opponents saw his 1929 record include thirteen defeats and four draws. Campaigning as a welterweight, four of his defeats cane in a four-month period against Albert Johnson, who stopped the Sunderland man twice. Johnson was the brother of the famous Len from Manchester, who struggled to get an official title fight because of his colour. During 1930, Casey made the step up to middleweight. Joe Lowther was the big-name round Leeds and, during that year, Jack and Lowther, from a well-known gypsy family, met five times. Joe won the first two in January at Hull and then Jack out-pointed Lowther on his own turf, at Brunswick Stadium. Joe, who won the Northern Area title during the year, retired Casey in four rounds at Preston, but when the action switched to Leeds again, five days before Christmas, Casey upset Lowther's supporters again by out-pointing their man.

In 1931, Casey came to the attention of a much wider audience. He retired the rated Archie Sexton in Manchester, who had beaten him the previous year in Sunderland in nine rounds. Then he got the better of local man George Willis, with whom he had drawn in Casey's first year of fighting and to whom he had lost twice in front of his own fans in Sunderland in 1929. Following that, he lost four on the trot, although it was no disgrace to be out-pointed by Fred Shaw twice and Jack Hood. The Sunderland hardman did not lose in his next sixteen outings, which included three, more fights against the Yorkshireman, Shaw. Twelve of his wins were inside the distance and news of the 'Sunderland Assassin', as he was now being labelled, had reached the ear of Jeff Dickson, the American promoter who had made his name in Paris and was now running promotions at the Royal Albert Hall. Dickson engaged Casey for an Anglo-French tournament (Casey's first appearance farther south than Barnsley). Dickson paid him £50 for his appearance, which proved value for money.

Marcel Thil, a recent victor over the American, Vince Dundee, in Paris and, until he lost the title in Milan in 1930 to Mario Bosisio, European champion, was matched with Jack. Thil had previously lost to Len Harvey and Jack Hood back in 1927 and had been beaten by Fred Shaw on his last British visit in 1929.

Jack Casey, Sunderland's tough-as-they-come,
British middleweight title challenger.

Delighted to be in the capital to collect his £50 for meeting the hard-boiled Frenchman, Casey spent all his time sightseeing.

Thil knew he was in for a fight when Casey connected with a fierce right, which split the Frenchman's eyebrow. With the strong possibility of a stoppage, Thil had to adopt caution and by the middle rounds the cut had stopped bothering him. The former European champion gave his man a pounding and, at the end of the contest, he expressed his astonishment at how much punishment Casey had taken without going down. The fight had not been one-way traffic though and the encounter helped make the 'Cast Iron' legend. Thil was a tough customer and, seven months later, the balding Frenchman was able to soak in the glory of being world champion. Thil beat the American 'Gorilla' Jones for the IBU version of the world middleweight title. Going on to avenge his defeats against Harvey and Hood, Thil later moved to light-heavyweight and won a second European title.

With his new fame, Casey hired a new manager – Walter Russell. His performance against Thil had put him in the British title frame and promoter John Paget was keen to put the match with champion Len Harvey on at the New St James Hall. There was no problem with Len, he was keen, but the British Boxing Board of Control, not in favour of title fights outside the capital, refused to sanction Casey as a contender. The fight went ahead as a non-title fight over fifteen rounds. Paget knew he had a sell-out contest with Jack's support coming

Jack Casey pictured with Len Harvey (right). Casey and the British champion took
part in two classic confrontations at Newcastle's New St James Hall, the second
fight with Harvey's title at stake.

predominantly from the mining fraternity. As usual, Casey came out and took
everything his opponent could throw at him and his style had Harvey boxing on
the retreat. Harvey was content to jab and clip his challenger from longer range.
The champion was content to spoil, a trait that led to hostility from the Casey
followers, who made so much noise that, on several occasions, neither fighter
heard the bell, and punches were thrown after the signal for the end of the round.
When he did come forward, Harvey showed what a superb ringmaster he was.
His speed was explosive. In round four, he produced a left hook followed by a

right to the jaw, which saw Casey go down in a professional ring for the first time ever. Casey was up immediately. The British champion knew already that a knockout was about as likely as Casey's frantic fans, who had been ordered to quieten down, changing sides. Leonard went back to boxing, content to wait for the openings instead of making them happen. In the last two rounds, Harvey again looked more like a champion. The consensus of opinion was that Harvey had done enough to win, though some of the partisan crowd disagreed. Afterwards, Casey praised his conqueror. Harvey replied that it had felt like fighting an iron man, adding, 'what do they feed you on? Filings?'

There was a ferocious fighter in Lancashire with a hard man reputation and, once Casey had moved up to the higher frame of middleweights, Jock McAvoy and the 'Sunderland Assassin' were on a collision course to meet. Just look at McAvoy's record from the first moment he donned a glove in 1927 until the end of 1932. He fought 104 times, won ninety-eight (of which sixty-nine failed to go the distance), drew one and lost two fights on disqualification. From his fifty-five fights from 1931 to 1934, Jock's three setbacks came against Len Harvey, in an unsuccessful tilt at Harvey's British middleweight title (a result he would avenge in 1935), and the fights against North-East ring men Paul McGuire and Jack Casey. Back in 1931, Casey publicly issued a challenge to McAvoy. The 'Sunderland Assassin' wondered: 'how can McAvoy call himself champion of the North (Jack had stopped Joe Lowther at Belle Vue to win the Northern Area middleweight title) when he had yet to face 'Cast Iron' Casey?' The fight had taken a backseat while McAvoy challenged Harvey. Both Manchester and Newcastle wanted to stage the fight and, in the end, the matchmaker at the Kings Hall at Belle Vue, Jack Madden, secured the rights. Droves of special trains, laid on by the railway, brought in the fans from Newcastle and Sunderland, who promptly backed their man at the bookmakers. The press hyped the fight and the remarks by Casey that he would knock McAvoy out turned it into a grudge fight.

The fight lived up to the billing and the two men slugged it out for fourteen rounds. McAvoy's crouching style made him a difficult man to hit and, with Jack forced to chase, it was Jock's counterpunching that totted up the points. In the middle rounds, the Northern Area champion tested the famous Casey chin. Jack's jaw withstood the fiercest punching. The tables were turned in round twelve when a good right dislodged McAvoy's gumshield. McAvoy, for a moment, looked like he might be toppled as a driving left knocked him off balance. In the following round, he was hanging on again with Casey unloading his heavy artillery. In the penultimate round Casey's supporters claimed a foul blow after a suspect low punch floored Jack. Another suspect low punch followed and this time referee Tom Gamble ruled out McAvoy. The fact that Casey was rising on his toes, accidental though the punch may have been, made it a foul blow. McAvoy had lost to Paul McGuire on a supposed low punch and had given the North-East man a hammering in the rematch, forcing him to retire. McAvoy clamoured for a rematch against Casey, but the new Northern Area champion did not need Jock McAvoy any more, for his win had secured an eliminator with Bethnal Green's Archie Sexton (whose son Dave was later to manage Manchester United) for Len Harvey's title.

Sexton came to the New St James Hall for his title chance, with the scores at one apiece and a draw between himself and Jack in previous encounters. Hundreds were turned away from the hall, unable to get into the overloaded venue. After a cautious start, Casey saw his chance and finished Sexton with a left hook, after weakening him with a flurry of heavy punches in round seven. Since their first fight at the beginning of 1932, Harvey had successfully defended against McAvoy, Len Johnson (not recognised by the British Boxing Board) and then lost in a challenge for Marcel Thil's world title at White City. The defeat against Thil was Harvey's first in Britain for five years. Jeff Dickson wanted to stage the fight in London, but Casey refused. There was only one venue for him and that was the New St James Hall, which he considered was a lucky venue. There had been efforts to stage the fight in Casey's hometown either at the Sunderland Empire or the Regal Cinema (built on the site of the old Holmeside Stadium). But John Paget's £800 bid took the fight to Newcastle and, at prices ranging from a guinea to 5s, the canny Paget had no problems in selling out the venue. Keen to impress officials from London, Paget had taps and running water with basins in each corner. There was a moment of levity when Harvey's basin refused to work and a plumber had to be sent for after round one. Referee Arthur S. Myers made it clear from the opening round that the excessive holding, particularly by Harvey, which had marred the first fight between the pair, would not be tolerated.

From the first round, the champion noted the improvement of his challenger. Some of the crudeness was no longer apparent and Casey now projected science in his repertoire without losing any of his power; the champion knew that, from the first round, it would be one of his hardest fights. Harvey got the better of the early rounds though and his left lead peppered away at Casey's chin. But, like other Casey opponents, the champion felt he was hitting a brick wall. In round six, Harvey engineered an opening and tried to finish it with a solid right. The hook had Jack rocking and two more good punches had the same effect. Casey's recovery was instant and the champion had to re-plan his strategy. Harvey's efforts had seen him bruise his right hand, with the result that most of his attacking work was now down to the left, with the right used sparingly in defence.

Jack's sheer aggressiveness won him the middle rounds and, when Harvey elected to join Jack in toe-to-toe combat, the crowd went wild. Harvey out boxed his challenger in rounds ten and eleven. Mid-way through round twelve, Casey produced the punch the crowd had been waiting for. Harvey was caught flush on the chin and was in big trouble. It looked as if Jack was only one punch away from becoming the new champion. As he moved in to deliver the coup de grace, Len smiled back, which caused Jack to hesitate for a split second and, almost as quickly, the moment was gone as the champion feinted and slid along the ropes out of danger. Harvey was skilful enough to make sure the 'Sunderland Assassin' never got another chance. Encouraged by the crowd, Casey gave it everything he had in the final round. Harvey, one of the greatest of the inter-war champions, showed his class by keeping the challenger at bay right up to the end. The crowd accepted and acknowledged the decision that allowed Len Harvey to keep his crown. Casey did find support in some areas – sparring partner Jim Ainsley was among the local fighters who thought Jack had deserved to win. Harvey defended again but lost to Jock McAvoy. Jack's direction, like his two rivals at the top, was an eventual move to the light-heavy brigade.

With his popularity in Sunderland at its height, Jack opened a gym and boxing school, managed by his father. With the world title at stake, there was a lot of talk of a return with Marcel Thil and a possible trip to America, a country that Harvey had not found to his liking. Neither event occurred and Archie Potts, in his book on Casey, related that Jack, ill advisedly, neglected the London rings (his only real fight there had been against Thil). For the next couple of years, at a time when he was at his peak, he did not advance. The chance to gain a second title fight evaporated at Belle Vue when, as the support to McAvoy *v.* Harvey, Jack lost to his old rival, Archie Sexton. Archie out-pointed him and it was the Londoner who went on to challenge the new champion McAvoy.

After tryouts in 1933, Casey moved into the light-heavyweight ranks during 1934 and, as light-heavies always seem to do to make a name, he was not against entering the ring with seasoned heavyweights. Hartlepool had an up and coming heavyweight called Jack London, whose route would eventually take him to the British heavyweight title. Casey conceded inches in height and two stones in weight to the twenty-year-old in their first meeting at the Engineers Club in West Hartlepool and, as seemed consistent with open-air shows, the rain poured down. It was a nothing fight for Casey, who had only been tempted by the big purse. It looked like a sensation was in the making for the rain soaked Hartlepool crowd, who witnessed Casey visiting the canvas twice, the second time in round ten. London was well ahead on points, but then with the impossible seemingly attainable (a Casey knockout), young Jack was forced to retire to his corner with a head injury. Casey's chin had had the last laugh after all.

Casey lost five of his nineteen fights of 1934 and there were several notable scalps. Two top-of-the-bill fights in Newcastle in the space of two weeks saw disqualifications handed out to Jack's opponents for persistent holding. Reggie Meen, who had been floored as early as round two, and Canadian light-heavyweight champion Charlie Belenger, who had gone the distance in the United States with the likes of Mickey Walker and Maxie Rosenbloom, both had their fights terminated in the seventh round. Casey out-pointed Tommy Farr, the Welsh light-heavyweight champion, who would earn his own branch of world fame with his performance against Joe Louis later in the decade.

Another creditable points win performance, when Jack weighed in at not much above middleweight, came against George Slack, the Doncaster heavyweight who held the Northern Area heavyweight title and was mentor to Bruce Woodcock. Successive defeats to German heavyweight, Erich Seelig, Canadian Paul Schaeffer and Manuel Abrew, a coloured heavyweight from Edinburgh, did not help Casey's claims for a tilt at the British light-heavyweight title, which was vacant after Len Harvey had relinquished it. Tommy Farr and Eddie Phillips met for the vacant title in 1935.

By the time 1935 dawned Jack Casey was past his prime. Fighting against heavyweights and five successive defeats, the last against the improved Jack London in the return, saw his retirement in May. Casey, like many fighters have done after hanging up their gloves, took over a pub. It did well at first, but Jack was a soft touch for hangers-on and started to lose money. He made a comeback the following year at twenty-nine years of age. He failed to set the world alight in his short return, which was curtailed by the war. His last fight was in 1942, when, coming in badly overweight, he tipped the scales at 14 stone 2 pounds. Ill health dogged him in later life and he passed away in 1980.

Boxing today often lacks the characters it had in its heyday. The North East, during the thirties, had not just one of the biggest men, but in 'Cast Iron' Casey they had one of the hardest men ever to don gloves in a British ring.

Charlie McDonald

At a time when a black man was a rare sight round the North East, the fighting fraternity in Sunderland took Charlie McDonald to heart. Charlie took each fight as it came, never caring who he fought. In reality, there was no other way because, as Len Johnson, a more successful boxer than Charlie, found, even for British born boxers, there was a colour bar existing in British title stakes. Early in his career, Charlie had the misfortune to take part in a bout that produced a fatal ending. It was said that when he was persuaded back into the ring, his right hand was never thrown again with power.

The son of William McDonald from St Vincent, Charlie was born in Sunderland after his father settled in the area and married a local girl. McDonald senior had boxed for money and later kept a gym frequented by local sportsman in Hendon. The third son, Charlie had early ambitions to follow his father into the ring and, despite the fact that good fighters in the North East were commonplace, McDonald junior took to the sport like a duck to water. Duggie Morton looked after a stream of local fighters and, in his first year in the sport, the young coloured boxer quickly graduated from six to fifteen-rounders.

One of his early setbacks, in 1926, came at the hands of 'Gunner' Ainsley, who usually boxed at around 12 stone and fought light-heavies and heavies. By the following year, McDonald had progressed enough to beat the former artilleryman, who would give Jack London a lot of help in his early days, twice.

In November 1927, Charlie met twenty-year-old Barnsley boxer Dick Roughley at an Arthur Heslop promotion at Leeds National Sporting Club. Trained by Charlie Glover, Roughley was already a veteran of over eighty fights. The fifteen-round contest saw both men take and give heavy blows and, in the final round, with Charlie getting the upper hand, Roughley went down for a six and then a nine count. When he rose the second time a straight left sent him towards the ropes, where the Barnsley youngster's head seemed to bounce off the bottom rung on the way down. Referee Ben Green stopped the fight and Roughley was taken to Leeds General Infirmary, where he died three days later, never having regained consciousness. The court hearing, proving the fight was not a prize-fight (no money deal between the fighters or their camps), returned a verdict of death by misadventure. The post mortem was unable to decide whether the punch or the fall had helped kill Roughley and Charlie, who attended both inquiries, was cleared of any blame. The Sunderland man was so upset afterwards, that he vowed never to fight again. Persuaded that he was not to blame, Charlie eventually returned to the ring, but never with the same punching power.

The 3,000-capacity Holmeside Stadium, which had been Sunderland's premier venue since its opening in 1920, was condemned to be knocked down and, with the advent of the talking pictures, was to be rebuilt as a cinema and dancehall. For the last ever promotion at the venue, in May 1930, the promoters, the Black Brothers, wanted to go out with a bang, with the cream of Sunderland's boxers meeting each other. This meant Duggie Parker boxing Billy Smith and Charlie meeting his fellow middleweight Jack Casey. Duggie Morton did not approve; he also managed Jack and did not want his two main assets slugging it out with each other (in the month prior to the fight Casey had lost to Scottish middleweight Sandy McKenzie in the second fight of the opening night of the New St James Hall in Newcastle. The old stadium had closed down in 1929 and the new hall was able to hold 5,000 instead of 3,000). The Casey v. McDonald fight was an anticlimax. Having sparred hundreds of rounds together, the two men knew each other too well. The pair had too much respect for each other and, with the fight always likely to go to the distance, Charlie was a comfortable winner on points. It was the end of an era for boxing on Wearside. The demise of the Sunderland stadium left the New St James Hall as the premier fight venue in the north.

A fortnight later, Morton accepted an engagement with a boxer on the verge of becoming Britain's greatest ringman of the inter-war period. It was not exactly the ideal preparation, travelling down to London, the day before the fight, on a motorbike with his second riding pillion, but Charlie was not going to miss the opportunity of appearing at a top London venue.

It was Len Harvey's first appearance at Premierland in what was essential a warm up for his forthcoming fight with the American, Dave Shade. There had been talk of Jeff Dickson, the American promoter, who was by now making a big impact in Britain after early disappointment in this country, arranging a fight for Harvey with the world middleweight champion, Mickey Walker. Both parties wanted too much money and the encounter with Shade at the Royal Albert Hall was Len's ticket to fight in the United States. Len, who would eventually move up to light-heavyweight and heavyweight with great success, had been undefeated since 1927, when Len Johnson had beaten him at the 'Ring' in Blackfriars. The year before Harvey had won the British and British Empire middleweight titles and was already the proud owner of an outright Lonsdale Belt. Charlie's performance against the champion failed to go past the second round. In the first round, he looked to have the qualities to go the distance. At the start of round two, Harvey knocked away his left lead and cut loose with a big swing to the body. The punch was good enough to finish poor Charlie and

Charlie McDonald, Sunderland's black
middleweight..

the 'Pride of Sunderland' was counted out. Harvey went on to beat Shade, but did not set America alight. His style was unsuitable; Len lost all his three fights there and all his later success would come in his home country.

Two West Yorkshiremen were contemporaries of McDonald. Charlie had the edge over Leeds fighter Joe Lowther (Northern Area middleweight champion 1930–31), losing only once in seven meetings. But he only beat Saltaire's Fred Shaw, the man who would earn his own fame by beating European and later world champion, Marcel Thil, once and drew two out of seven contests.

In January 1931, a couple of weeks after out-pointing Mick McGuire's brother Paul, at the New St James Hall, Charlie went fifteen rounds with Jock McAvoy, the Manchester based fighter with a reputation as one of boxing's most fearsome punchers. McAvoy, who took Joe Lowther's title later in the year and who would challenge Len Harvey for his titles, went into the fight at Liverpool Stadium on the back of fifteen straight wins (eight inside the distance). The result was never really in doubt and, after his performance against Harvey, Charlie was satisfied to go the distance with a fighter rated as a big rival for Harvey's titles. Fourteen months later, Jock unsuccessfully challenged the champion. Jock's turn would come. For after another year of seeing off all the title aspirants, he took Harvey's titles in the return. In the period between his fights with McDonald and Harvey, Jock's only setback was against Newcastle's Paul McGuire, on a four-round disqualification. This was always a possibility with McAvoy's fiery temper.

It was a result that Jock corrected in a rematch, when he stopped McGuire in two rounds at Blackpool. Charlie's rematch with McGuire came a couple of weeks after his defeat against McAvoy at Liverpool; McGuire out-pointed him over fifteen rounds at Middlesbrough's Winter Gardens.

In the summer of 1932, Charlie met West Hartlepool's light-heavyweight, Jack London, at catchweight. McDonald weighed in just 4 pounds short of 2 stone lighter, in front of a full house at the Redworth Street Stadium. London, who had out-pointed Paul McGuire in his previous fight, thought his weight advantage would swing the fight for him, but he could not best the Sunderland man's experience. Charlie boxed London into the canvas with scoring counters and even Jack's fiercest Hartlepool supporters could not claim that their man had beaten Charlie. At the same time, no one could visualise that, thirteen years later, in 1944, London would out-point Freddie Mills to win British and British Empire heavyweight titles. Six months later, London and Charlie met again. The improvement in Jack was apparent. He had only lost one of five fights in between the two contests and, although Charlie did well again, London edged the verdict.

Del Fontaine, who had won the Canadian middleweight title back in 1926 and then fought in America, where he had met, among others, Mickey Walker, who had knocked him out in four rounds in 1930 (it was Walkers twenty-ninth win in an unbeaten run of forty-four), came to England in 1932. Most of the Canadian's early fights were at Blackfriars, but he did venture north and met Charlie at Leeds. Fontaine was still a fair boxer and he knocked Charlie out in four rounds. The Canadian did, however, overstay his time in England, losing too many fights and becoming a punch bag for even ordinary British middleweights. Later, he was convicted of killing a girlfriend and hanged at Wandsworth Prison.

South African Eddie Maguire was another boxer who stayed on in England. His career had started in Johannesburg in 1929 and, two years later, he became his country's middleweight champion. On his arrival in England, great things must have been expected, for former world flyweight champion, Jimmy Wide, was appointed to look after him. Eddie lost his first fight in England to Jack Casey and met Charlie in his sixth at the New St James Hall. Charlie confirmed the South African's fifth defeat in six fights. Casey then knocked the South African out in three rounds in Newcastle, but there was to be some improvement because, before the end of 1933, Maguire out-pointed Casey at the New St James Hall and drew with him in a fourth meeting at Hull.

Charlie's career came to an end in 1936 and he retired in style by winning all of his fights that year. He was not lost from the local fight scene; he was a popular face at later promotions in the area where they had taken to him as one of their own.

'Seaman' Tommy Watson

Of all the success that came the way of North-East boxers during the thirties, few fight enthusiasts would disagree that the greatest feat came from the fighting fists of the Byker featherweight, 'Seaman' Tommy Watson. Nel Tarleton was deified on Merseyside: his defensive qualities were such that he was considered unbeatable, especially in front of his adorning Liverpudlians. Watson not only came back to the North with Tarleton's title, but he also crowned his career by travelling to New York to fight another great champion in 'Kid Chocolate' for the world featherweight title.

Born in 1908 and one of nine children, Tommy sold papers on street corners from the age of eight. Another eight years later and the youngster from Byker joined the Royal Navy. Although he had experienced local gymnasiums, it was in the Navy where his pugilistic career began to take shape. Home on leave a year later, he made his pro debut in Newcastle. An unbeaten run, coupled with appearances at Blackfriars, brought him to the attention of London promoter, Alec Lambert. Tommy signed for Lambert in 1928 and two years later 'Seaman' Watson left the Navy as its lightweight champion with the confidence that he could emulate Lambert's predictions of becoming a British champion.

After six years of campaigning, Watson's only defeats had been two setbacks against Bristol's George Rose until he met Liverpool favourite, Dom Volante, at the Royal Albert Hall in the Byker man's biggest payday so far. Volante was a stablemate of the British featherweight champion Nel Tarleton and the Italian-Merseysider did what no other boxer had done in over sixty professional appearances: he stopped 'Seaman' Tommy Watson. In the first phase of his career, Tommy had only boxed eleven times in his native North East. After the Volante defeat he was back treading the boards at St James Hall. Wins over local rivals Benny Sharkey and Duggie Parker and two wins over the Belgian champion Francois Machtens, one of them in London, restored Tommy to title contention. Watson was on hand to watch the champion, Tarleton, in action when the Liverpudlian fought Sharkey in Newcastle. Benny was outclassed, but it was a good night for Tommy, for he was able to collect some valuable notes for future reference. Soon afterwards, he learned he was to meet Nella for his title in the champion's backyard. With Volante stopping Watson, Tarleton had some background on his challenger. Nella, though, might not have been aware that when the former seaman fought Volante, he had been suffering badly from tonsillitis and had refused to withdraw because he wanted to keep in the title frame. There was further information for Tarleton: in his last fight prior to meeting the champion, Tommy beat his sparring partner, the Welshman, Phineas John.

Although only two men had beaten him in eighty-nine fights and he had earned every right to challenge for the title, no one gave 'Seaman' Watson much chance, especially on Nella's own home ground where the task was thought to be an impossible mission. Johnny Best's new Liverpool Stadium hosted the fight. The famous stadium, throughout its history, became known as the 'graveyard of champions' and 10 November 1932 was one of those nights. Watson upset all the odds to beat a great champion with a tremendous display. This was Watson's chance. He might never get another and he gave everything to take the runaway favourite's title. The result was not popular in the stadium, but Watson was impervious; the win had opened up new doors for the new British featherweight champion. Tarleton had a fight pencilled in against the Cuban world champion 'Kid Chocolate' at the famous Madison Square Gardens, but because he was no longer the champion, the fight was in tatters.

After a hero's welcome, and a couple of stoppage wins in his beloved North East to round off a successful 1932, Tommy's manager announced that it had been arranged for Watson to meet the Cuban world champion in New York in the new year.

Before Watson could sail for America for the fight, the news broke that the New York State Athletic Commission had vetoed the fight because they were unsure whether the British man was a credible challenger for the world title. Watson still sailed to America in an attempt to prove his worthiness in a tryout contest to impress officials. While the British press were arguing that Tommy's win over Tarleton guaranteed him his chance, the New York authorities appeared to be influenced by sportswriter Dan Parker. Apparently, six years earlier, the State Athletic Commission had decided that any non-American must fight in one of the clubs to prove he was worthy of engaging in a main bout at the New York Gardens. The rule had come about after the fight between Fidel La Barba and Elky Clark in 1927 for the world flyweight title. Tommy proved he was capable of meeting the Cuban champion, when, in front of authorities and press, he engaged in three, two-round sparring matches against selected opponents. Satisfied Watson could give 'Kid Chocolate' a contest, the now arranged fight had to be put back because the Cuban had to return to Havana where it was alleged he had not obtained a permit to enter the United States. Reluctant to

'Seaman' Tommy Watson, the man from Byker who ended the title reign of legend Nel Tarleton and took his place in a fight at the world title at Madison Square Gardens against the crack Cuban 'Kid Chocolate'.

return home without a fight, Tommy's management team arranged a fight with the former champion La Barba, who only one month earlier had gone fifteen rounds in an attempt at 'Chocolate's' title. A win over the former flyweight would settle any doubters.

La Barba had quit boxing, after his success in 1927, to return to university. Losing money in the 1929 Wall Street Crash, Fidel had returned to boxing as a bantam. After early upsets against 'Chocolate' and 'Kid' Francis, La Barba came back with a vengeance. He beat the likes of Earl Mastro, Petey Sarron, Bushy Graham and 'Chocolate' in a rematch and, after four wins over Tommy Paul, he challenged 'Battling' Battalino for the world featherweight title in 1931. He lost the fifteen-round points verdict to Battalino, who held the then undisputed title, before challenging for 'Kid Chocolate's' New York version. 'Chocolate' had gained revenge in the fight, but nine out of eleven newspapermen thought La Barba had won it. La Barba had had a recent setback in a non-title bout against Tommy Paul, who was recognised as the National Boxing Association champion. La Barba, who saw the fight as a stepping stone for another clash with 'Chocolate', set a blistering pace in front of the 11,000 Madison Square Garden boxing fans. After a quiet start, Tommy, while conscious of La Barba's favourite left hook, evened up as the twelve-round fight reached the middle stages. The Americans warmed to the British boxer, who was quickly gaining comparisons to 'Kid' Berg, the other British ringman who fought like an American. Tommy took the verdict, as both fighters gave their all in the final rounds. There were no complaints from Fidel, Watson had beaten him at his own game of in-fighting and the crowd's reaction had guaranteed big interest in a fight with 'Kid Chocolate'.

A few months later, after Tommy had returned to the North East for another hero's welcome, the news came that the 'Kid Chocolate' fight was on, after the 'Cuban Bon Bon' as he was widely nicknamed (his real name was Eligo Sardinas) had been allowed back into the United States. Arranged for May 1933, the fight was put back another week, when 'Chocolate' was supposedly ill with a bad stomach.

Born in the ghetto district of El Cierro in Havana, the young street fighter, nicknamed 'Kid Chocolate', racked up a hundred straight wins as an amateur, including a staggering eighty-six knockouts. Luis Gutierrez, who worked as a sports editor, realised his potential. He duly became his manager and took the young Cuban to America's boxing capital, New York, in 1928, where he quickly became a sensation. 'Chocolate' returned to Havana the following year to win his first title, the 'Coloured Featherweight Championship of the World', by beating Chick Suggs. Back in New York, 37,000 watched 'Chocolate' fight Al Singer at the Polo Grounds and, during the same year, he beat Bushy Graham in front of 16,000 at Madison Square Gardens. The Graham fight had been proposed for the world bantam title but the NYAC had refused sanction. The fight caused a riot because 1,000 counterfeit tickets had been sold and legitimate punters could not get into their seats.

It was an Englishman who took his unbeaten record. There were 36,565 present at the Polo Grounds to see 'Chocolate' take on world junior welterweight champion Jack 'Kid' Berg. Arguments over a stipulated weight arrangement saw 'Chocolate' enter the ring at least 10 pounds lighter than his opponent. Despite the disadvantage, 'Chocolate' put up a tremendous battle. Berg edged it and his 168-fight (amateur and pro) unbeaten record went. The Cuban was so upset that he broke down in the ring and wept. After the Berg defeat and a further loss to La Barba, 'Kid Chocolate' was back in shape to challenge 'Battling' Battalino for the world featherweight title in 1930. Battalino was lucky to survive the first round and at the end the officials gave it to Battalino, though the knowledgeable crowd at the Gardens and the press saw it otherwise. A title did come in 1931, when Benny Bass was battered in seven rounds in Philadelphia and 'Chocolate' was crowned the world junior lightweight champion. In a bid to win a second world title, the lightweight champion Tony Canzoneri beat him on a split decision. It was a great battle and the crowd, with whom the Cuban was a great favourite, showed their disapproval at the decision. Berg beat him again on a split decision, in a non-title fight, before Battalino's resignation of his title saw 'Kid Chocolate' matched with Lew Feldman in a fight for the vacant world featherweight championship and the 'Kid's' world junior title. There was no argument about this one as 'Chocolate' knocked out Feldman to reclaim his title.

La Barba was favoured in some quarters to take his new title. This was a close affair. While most of the press went for the challenger, two judges went for the champion and the third judge saw it as a draw.

'Seaman' Tommy Watson was next on the agenda and, once the Cuban's permit problems were sorted out, the fight went ahead, with an agreement made that if 'Chocolate' lost, there was to be a return with Tommy within sixty days. Gutierrez was not even contemplating defeat, he already had 'Chocolate's' next two title fights arranged: against Tony Canzoneri and the NBA claimant Freddie Miller.

Not surprisingly the champion was 2-1 favourite, in a fight attended by 13,836 at the famous Gardens. Certainly not in awe of the champion, Tommy won applause in the opening round for his close work. 'Chocolate' threw plenty of hooks and uppercuts; some were wild, but enough found the mark to give the champion the first round. The second was closer, but there was concern about the way 'Chocolate' was finding the target with big rights. Watson went straight onto the attack in round three. 'Chocolate' took the pressure and had the crowd on their feet as he finished the round with a barrage of heavy punches. There was better to come from the Englishman in the next rounds. He shook the champion and for the first time in the fight he had 'Kid Chocolate' backing off. Watson did well again in round six, although there was a moment when lefts by 'Chocolate' made ringsiders wonder whether Tommy might fall.

Perked up by his corner for letting Watson back into the fight, round seven saw a busier champion. 'Chocolate' out boxed his opponent and his two-fisted attack troubled the man from Byker. Watson was by now feeling the power of the Cuban's punches and, in round ten, 'Kid Chocolate' put him down. Tommy won applause from the American audience for the way he fought back, but it was obvious to his handlers that he needed to produce something special to take the title. The Cuban started to play to the crowd in round eleven and looked odds on for keeping his title. There was no surrender from Tommy though. He was participating in a once-in-a-lifetime fight and, having his best round since round four, he staggered the Cuban in round twelve. Hooks started to find their mark and there was a moment when 'Chocolate' looked vulnerable, but Tommy elected not to follow up and the chance was quickly gone. Round thirteen was another good round for Watson and suddenly he was back in the fight. Round fourteen was split and Tommy, as 'Chocolate' tired, looked to take the last round. A unanimous decision saw the champion keep his title, but there had been a lot in the fight that Tommy's native North East could be proud of. No one had given him a chance. He thought he had won himself, but American referees always seemed to see fights differently.

After his great performance against 'Chocolate' in New York, the former Byker seaman was sanctioned by the Boxing Board to meet Chocolate again. With the 'Cuban Bon Bon' touring Europe in late 1933, promoters were offering the world champion purses of up to £3,000 to defend his title against the British champion, in London. 'Chocolate' had won what was considered a very close fight, by a unanimous decision from the American judges. When Tommy's name did not figure on a list of possible opponents, the Cuban's manager Luis Gutierrez stated that he did not want his man meeting Tommy in England because he was frightened that British interpretation of the fight, had it gone the distance, might see his man lose his title. When it was seen that François Machtens from Belgium, a two times Watson victim, was matched with 'Kid Chocolate' in Barcelona and rumours were heard about circulating how unimpressive the Cuban was, perhaps there was more than worry about than a British referee in a rematch with Tommy. When more stringent efforts were made to get the fight on, it was found the Cuban and his entourage had slipped back to America.

In the United States, Freddie Miller was the big name on the featherweight scene. His win over Tommy Paul had given him the NCA version of the title and the Cincinnati southpaw's management were keen to bring Miller to England to fight Tommy. While negotiations lingered, Tommy was forced to return to action, to mixed fortunes. In his hero's return to the North East, he again proved the master of his main local rival, Benny Sharkey. But when he met Leeds fighter, Sonny Lee, a defeat was recorded. Tommy, who bitterly disputed the referee's decision was thrown out in round two for an alleged low punch. There was further disappointment, when a fight in London with the world bantam champion, 'Panama' Al Brown, failed to materialise at the last minute: Brown had left the country for Algiers.

With 'Chocolate' out of the frame, having lost his title to Tony Canzoneri, before electing to box permanently as a lightweight and with Miller still in America, Watson returned to defences of his British featherweight title. Making his first appearance in Scotland in front of 11,000 patriotic Scots at Kelvin Hall, Watson beat local challenger Johnny McMillan in fifteen rounds. After further wins against notables like Jimmy Walsh, François Machtens and Dick Corbett, came the return with the man from whom Tommy had taken the title, Nel Tarleton. Since Tommy had done what many considered impossible twenty months ago, Tarleton had toured Australia before returning to challenge for his old title. With his body punching, which many thought would be too much for Tarleton, Watson was the favourite everywhere except on Merseyside. A 15,000 crowd at Anfield saw both men have their moments, until the fight reached the fourteenth round with Watson holding a slight lead. As the boxers closed together, Watson went down after what looked like an unintentional head butt. The champion rose at eight, but needed all his skills to keep Tarleton at bay until the end of the round. As the last round commenced, Tarleton saw the winning line and went to regain his title. The result was not popular in some quarters and several reporters argued that Watson had done enough to earn an outright Lonsdale Belt.

Two months later, Tarleton, with the right credentials now he was British champion again, stepped in the ring with world champion, Freddie Miller, and went fifteen rounds in a valiant attempt to win Liverpool's first world title. While pundits argued that Tommy Watson, who lost his chance to fight for the title with Miller, would have beaten the American southpaw, it was announced that Watson would campaign in future as a lightweight.

A year on, Watson had won eliminators against Sonny Lee and Tommy Spiers to fight for Jack 'Kid' Berg's lightweight title. With Miller more or less permanently based in Britain, Johnny Best, the promoter at Liverpool Stadium, was able to get Tarleton another title crack. Freddie repeated his hard-fought win over Nella and, only a fortnight later, Miller stepped into the ring with Tommy Watson in a ten-round non-title fight. This should have been the fight for the world title a year earlier. There was a big carrot dangling for the man from Byker if he could beat Freddie. The champion's manager, Pete Reilly, had cabled Best to say that if Tommy won, he would be able to offer him a shot at world lightweight champion Tony Canzoneri, in the United States. The rain, which often ruined Johnny Best's outside promotions at Anfield came down in copious quantities, limiting the Watson *v.* Miller clash to 12,000 spectators. Rain or no rain, everyone stayed to the end. Freddie, who was more popular on Merseyside than Watson, took the ten-round points decision. It was badly received and the American was booed from some sections of the rain-soaked crowd. Watson had done well in the first two rounds and a short right had put Miller down for a three count near the end of round two. Tommy tried to follow up the advantage, but Miller was ready for him and, twice, right hooks to the jaw reversed the situation. In round four, Watson looked finished, when Miller's impressive punching power sent him to the floor for a nine count. Tommy survived the count and came back strongly in the last three rounds. The crowd were under the assumption that Watson's late rally had turned the tables, but most of the press thought the decision was correct. However, there was an instant clamour for a rematch.

John Mortimer, who had a long association with Watson, particularly in his fights in the North East, immediately issued a challenge to Miller for a return with a side stake of £500. Miller accepted and announced that he would back himself. The rematch was fixed for Anfield a month later. Between the two fights, continuing the elimination series to meet 'Kid' Berg, Tommy beat Frankie Brown.

Miller's instructions from Reilly, who was back in America, had been to not risk a knockout, but to win on points. Those orders were soon forgotten, when Miller's attack forced Tommy onto the defensive. Both men ended the opening round trading punches, a situation which Tommy welcomed. The intensity of Tommy's attack drove Miller back and overconfidence proved costly. As Watson rushed in again, a slight drop of the guard saw Miller's right send Watson across the ring. His head hit the ring floor with a heavy bang and, for the first time in his professional career, Tommy Watson was counted out.

The world title dream was over and, at twenty-seven years of age, there was speculation that Tommy would hang up his gloves. A final eliminator with George Daley was supposed to be his next fight for the lightweight title. Both fighters turned down the offered purse and then met on a Jeff Dickson promotion. Tommy lost on points; it was his last fight.

He did return to the sport for a while as a referee but, like many former fighters, he became involved in the licensing trade. He stayed true to his North-East roots and died in 1971, aged sixty-two.

Benny Sharkey

North-East boxing writers John Jarrett and Owen Hughes referred to Sharkey, in book and article form, as the 'Wrecker of Champions'. Indeed, throughout his career the rugged Jewish featherweight was that and more. But, despite his achievements against past and present champions of world and British title stature, Benny was fighting in an era when there was so much competition that no title fight, not even at Area level, came his way.

Like his Sunderland rival, Duggie Parker, Benny was born in Scotland, in Glasgow in 1911, and moved to Byker as a youngster. His family background was the Jewish quarter of Leeds and it was in the West Riding city that his father, Leon Goldwater, adopted the name of American boxer, Tom Sharkey, and earned his own boxing reputation, firstly in the local booth and later around the country. Sons followed fathers into the ring and from Benny's older brothers, Freddie and Willie, the latter was the best-known in North-East rings. One of nine children, Benny was an apprentice bricklayer at fourteen and first began to take the fight game seriously when his father summoned him to novice competitions in Byker. The bug bit and, once it was seen as a way of earning an extra bob or two, there were enough small-time promotions for Benny to appear four or five times a week in four-rounders. By the time he was eighteen and known as a fighter who would give his all, he was as popular as anyone in Newcastle. Soon his name had spread to other boxing centres like Leeds and Liverpool.

In a fight at Liverpool, that produced as much blood as to be found in a butcher's shop, Sharkey stood toe-to-toe with Irish featherweight champion, Packy McParland, to record his first win over a big-name opponent. John Paget promised a big fight at the New St James Hall and produced the goods when British bantam champion, Teddy Baldock, travelled north to Newcastle. Baldock had been inactive because of attempts to match him with world champion 'Panama' Al Brown in New York. When Brown's handlers matched him with French champion, Eugene Huat, in Paris instead, Baldock agreed to meet the Newcastle fighter he knew little about in September 1930. Teddy had, in fact, claimed a version of the world title in 1927, when the American claimant, Archie

Bell, lost a thriller on points to the London bantam at the Royal Albert Hall. The fight elevated Baldock to the status of an icon in southern England, although the title was not recognised abroad. Teddy lost his title to the South African, Willie Smith, although even that result was in dispute, because Baldock came in 2 pounds over the limit.

There was intense rivalry in London between Baldock and Alf 'Kid' Pattenden. The famed boxing scribe, Gilbert Odd, wrote about it as the 'East End bantam war'. The fight lived up to the billing and was hailed as Baldock's greatest triumph. The champion came to Newcastle boasting a record of only two defeats in seventy-four fights over nine years in the ring. But, despite Baldock's credentials, there was still a flutter from the Geordies on their man. Benny went about the fight in the only way he knew, taking the fight to the champion, who had the advantage of three years and was 3 inches taller. With the crowd ranting from the first punch, Sharkey's aggression, coupled with his hand speed, had the Londoner backing off. Baldock seemed content to let Sharkey go ahead in the early rounds, but, by round six, he decided more effort was needed. For the first time the Newcastle crowd glimpsed Baldock's champion qualities as he drove Benny to the ropes. There was no surrender from Sharkey. He produced a stunning left and Teddy, for a while, looked in trouble. Baldock upped the pace but Benny stayed with him. Experience began to tell and in rounds eleven and twelve Sharkey suffered the worst of the action. The last round would prove decisive. While onlookers pondered whether Teddy had done enough to wipe out the arrears, Benny gave it everything. It was enough to give him the verdict. The crowd went delirious at the victory and, after the fight, when Benny, as per usual, had walked home to Byker, he found the street outside his home lined with fans.

Sharkey's win put him on the national stage and the American, Jeff Dickson, captivating London audiences with the in-depth quality of his big promotions, booked Benny to fight 'Kid' Socks at the Royal Albert Hall. Sharkey's points win was impressive enough that Dickson matched the Newcastle bantam with Dick Corbett the following month. Benny failed to produce his earlier form and was out-pointed. Former flyweight Emile Pladner, who had moved up to bantam, was the next London opponent and Benny boosted any title aspirations he boasted, by beating Pladner over eight rounds and adding the Frenchman to a growing list of rated opponents he had conquered.

Obviously there was interest in bringing big names to Newcastle, but, for the fight fan in the North East, the ring battles against local rivals were the real nitty-gritty. One local paper was shouting the worth of Sharkey and another, in almost deliberate opposition, the case for Winlanton's Billy Farrell. The hype worked and 15,000 were drawn to Brough Park to witness the 'Cock of the North' encounter. Jimmy Wilde was the third man in the ring and, in a fight that looked to be finishing early, a towel thrown into the ring saved Farrell from a knockout, when Billy could not cope with Benny's savagery.

Benny Sharkey, Newcastle's 'wrecker of champions'.

Brough Park, later in 1931, was the scene of the battle between Benny and 'Seaman' Tommy Watson. Tommy had accounted for his other local rival, having beaten Duggie Parker twice in the first three months of 1931 (he would complete a third victory after two clashes with Benny). Now with his record putting him in the frame for a British title fight, fellow Byker man, Benny Sharkey, who lived only a few streets away, was the last of the local men he needed to sweep aside in his search for a title fight. After his upset against the Liverpool fighter, Dom Volante, at the Royal Albert Hall (where Benny had restored local pride on the bill with his win over Pladner) Watson had out-pointed Frenchman, Julian Verbist, two weeks before he encountered Benny. Tommy was campaigning as a featherweight and, with Benny comfortable with the weight, the scene was set for another local battle royal.

The occasion tied in with the Gosforth Park race meeting. There was a big turnout but unfortunately heavy rain put a damper on the proceedings. Another famous boxer was in the ring: Owen Moran had led the British trail in America before the First World War. Moran had to ask for sawdust as both fighters struggled with the soaking wet canvas. Watson, who was the heavier man, produced the more direct punches on the night and his accuracy ensured he was the winner. Benny was keen for a rematch and everyone knew he would make a fight of it, knowing that the defeat had assured Watson's place above him in the pecking order for a title fight. Tommy stated that he was ready anytime and,

Line-up at St James Hall, 11 February 1935. Back row, left to right: Tom Henderson, Jerry Delaney, Pat Butler, George Biddles, Nat Sellars, George Bunter, Benny Caplan, Benny Huntman, J.J. Paget. Front row, left to right: Roy Mills, Benny Sharkey, Johnny Mack, Huig Huizenaar, Robert Disch.

St James Hall, Newcastle, 2 November 1936 – the night Sharkey was out-pointed by Johnny Cusick. Benny Sharkey is second from left, back row and Johnny Cusick is far right, back row. Also on the bill was Peter Miller (middle, front row) *v*. Jimmy Warick (right, front row).

frightened of another event ruined by downpour, John Paget staged the rematch at the New St James Hall two months after the first fight, in August 1931.

Both men prepared at the Bridge End Gym in Byker, Sharkey training in the afternoon to avoid Watson, who was 5-4 favourite for a fight advertised as for the 'Featherweight Title of the North'. The advantages that Tommy had held in the first fight carried him through to the second meeting. Watson matched his opponent's punching, aggressiveness and stamina and, as the rounds went by, it was apparent that Sharkey's only chance of victory was with a stoppage. He rattled Watson in round eight and again in the final round when he broke through with shots to the body. Alas, for the second time, 'Seaman' Tommy Watson was Benny's master.

Pleased to come through the Watson fights unscathed, Benny sailed for South Africa. He had had a fight arranged for sometime in Johannesburg against Willie Smith, the country's featherweight champion, who had earlier claimed the world bantamweight title after his win against Teddy Baldock. He was out-pointed by Smith, but did record a win in his second fight in Africa, when he knocked out Johnny Bosman. The gap between Watson and Sharkey widened further in 1932. Like Tommy, Benny beat Duggie Parker a couple of times, but could not master François Machtens. The Belgian beat him twice during that year, whereas Tommy out-pointed Machtens twice inside twelve months and would record four wins out of four over the popular Belgian visitor. Benny dropped a decision to Nel Tarleton and in November, Tommy not only did what was thought impossible by defeating Nella in Liverpool, he took the Merseyside legend's place, in May 1933, in New York, in a challenge for the world title against Cuba's 'Kid Chocolate'.

On Watson's first fight back in England, Sharkey got another chance, when Tommy fulfilled his promise to meet Benny on his return. Sharkey was in good nick and had proved it the week prior with an accurate punching display to stop Billy Farrell. With Tommy being hot news since his performance in America, the local papers' daily bulletins added to the fight-fever, which not only swallowed Byker, but a big chunk of the North East. Again Watson had too much for Benny, although the Byker Jew did cause a commotion in round ten. In his usual style, Benny took the fight to the champion. Able to handle the pressure, Watson continually slowed Sharkey down with solid body shots. In the ninth round, Tommy became careless and Benny's right hook drove him to the ropes. Benny followed him in the next round and another right hook put Watson down. Tommy had the experience to get over the punch quickly and, after Benny had slowed down from his efforts, Watson took the points decision. It was undisputable.

The year 1933 was patchy for Benny. He was knocked out in four rounds by local rival Duggie Parker and dropped an unlucky decision at the Palace Theatre in Newcastle to Welshman Phineas John, whom he had beaten in 1931. He dropped and won decisions against the Glaswegian, Johnny McMillan, who

frightened of another event ruined by downpour, John Paget staged the rematch at the New St James Hall two months after the first fight, in August 1931.

Both men prepared at the Bridge End Gym in Byker, Sharkey training in the afternoon to avoid Watson, who was 5-4 favourite for a fight advertised as for the 'Featherweight Title of the North'. The advantages that Tommy had held in the first fight carried him through to the second meeting. Watson matched his opponent's punching, aggressiveness and stamina and, as the rounds went by, it was apparent that Sharkey's only chance of victory was with a stoppage. He rattled Watson in round eight and again in the final round when he broke through with shots to the body. Alas, for the second time, 'Seaman' Tommy Watson was Benny's master.

Pleased to come through the Watson fights unscathed, Benny sailed for South Africa. He had had a fight arranged for sometime in Johannesburg against Willie Smith, the country's featherweight champion, who had earlier claimed the world bantamweight title after his win against Teddy Baldock. He was out-pointed by Smith, but did record a win in his second fight in Africa, when he knocked out Johnny Bosman. The gap between Watson and Sharkey widened further in 1932. Like Tommy, Benny beat Duggie Parker a couple of times, but could not master François Machtens. The Belgian beat him twice during that year, whereas Tommy out-pointed Machtens twice inside twelve months and would record four wins out of four over the popular Belgian visitor. Benny dropped a decision to Nel Tarleton and in November, Tommy not only did what was thought impossible by defeating Nella in Liverpool, he took the Merseyside legend's place, in May 1933, in New York, in a challenge for the world title against Cuba's 'Kid Chocolate'.

On Watson's first fight back in England, Sharkey got another chance, when Tommy fulfilled his promise to meet Benny on his return. Sharkey was in good nick and had proved it the week prior with an accurate punching display to stop Billy Farrell. With Tommy being hot news since his performance in America, the local papers' daily bulletins added to the fight-fever, which not only swallowed Byker, but a big chunk of the North East. Again Watson had too much for Benny, although the Byker Jew did cause a commotion in round ten. In his usual style, Benny took the fight to the champion. Able to handle the pressure, Watson continually slowed Sharkey down with solid body shots. In the ninth round, Tommy became careless and Benny's right hook drove him to the ropes. Benny followed him in the next round and another right hook put Watson down. Tommy had the experience to get over the punch quickly and, after Benny had slowed down from his efforts, Watson took the points decision. It was undisputable.

The year 1933 was patchy for Benny. He was knocked out in four rounds by local rival Duggie Parker and dropped an unlucky decision at the Palace Theatre in Newcastle to Welshman Phineas John, whom he had beaten in 1931. He dropped and won decisions against the Glaswegian, Johnny McMillan, who fought Watson for his title in 1934 and defeated South African visitor Louis Botes.

In a busy 1934, in which he took part in thirty-one fights, he defeated local men Billy Charlton, Billy Sheldon and Jim Hurst and lost to Sheffield's boy boxing prodigy Frankie Barron, Johnny McGrory and a controversial decision to Italian Dominic Bernasconi, the European champion, whose record included wins over Johnny McGrory and Johnny King. The Italian had fought Al Brown for the world title, in a fight which saw Brown disqualified for persistent holding and then reinstated by the Italian Boxing Union and go on to retain his title. Benny looked to be heading for an easy win, when he appeared in distress. When his brother Willie rushed to help, his entry into the ring instantly gave the verdict to the Italian on the disqualification rule. The problem had been Benny's gumshield, which had become lodged in his throat.

Later in the year, John Paget had an option on American world featherweight champion Freddie Miller, who was on a barnstorming three-month Ministry of Labour permit tour. Averaging a fight a week, Miller was relaxing between fights on the golf course and, the day prior to meeting Benny, the southpaw champion played thirty-six holes on Newcastle Golf Course. Miller had come through a title defence with Nel Tarleton on his English debut and his fight with Sharkey was his fourth bout in eighteen days. Tommy Watson had witnessed Miller beat Tarleton and he predicted Benny would be the kind of scrapper to give the American a great fight. There were the usual problems with Americans over bandages and, in echoes of other visitors to British shores, Freddie wanted his money before he fought. Like Billy Charlton, who would encounter Freddie later, Benny had problems coping with Miller's southpaw style. Benny fought hard from the opening bell. Adept at foiling his opponent's rushes, Miller forced his man away and produced his own fireworks. A right feint followed by a left jab did the damage and poor Benny was counted out on his back, the first round not over. Benny had around thirty fights in 1935, winning two thirds of them and, in February the following year, he hit the headlines again when St James Hall lived up to its old reputation as the 'graveyard of champions'.

In the summer of 1935, the Spaniard, Balthazar Sangchili, who had come to fame with wins over 'Young' Perez and 'Kid' David, drew with 'Panama' Al Brown in a ten-round non-title fight. The result was enough for the Spanish promoters to move heaven and earth to get the reigning world champion to put his title on the line in a rematch in Valencia. Unable to turn down the fight, the thirty-two-year-old champion made a mistake by agreeing to a contest in the Spanish heat. Sangchili never gave him an inch and Brown, who was already weakened making the weight, for once could not make his 76-inch reach decisive. With both opponent and crowd giving him a rough ride, Brown's title went in the Spanish heat.

There were offers for the new world champion to go to America for a unification fight, but that was not in the immediate plans of the Sangchili handlers. A proposed title fight with Manchester's Johnny Cusick was knocked back by the British Boxing Board who considered the nineteen-year-old to be too short of experience. Instead the world champion came to Newcastle for what he presumably considered a routine non-title fight against a boxer who had already lost thirty-four fights out of 118. Sangchili prepared in Liverpool under Nel Tarleton and had the 'Liverpool Legend' in his corner. The increased prices to accommodate a world champion were not popular but those who thought Benny Sharkey was past his best were in for a shock. Rising to the occasion, Benny sent his man to his knees during round three. The Spaniard made the mistake of rising too early and Benny made him pay. Sangchili came back in the fourth, but the advantage was back with Benny in round five. Sharkey brought his uppercut back into play and Balthazar felt its power. The world champion adopted a different stance in round six, but it did not deter Benny. His left hand not only rattled up more points, but it visibly tired Sangchili. The Spaniard came back during round seven as both men had success with powerful blows. Round eight had the champion attempting to prove he was not beaten. But he was not making any real impression and it was becoming more obvious to everyone in the hall that Sangchili needed a knockout to win. Benny welcomed a 'tear up' and was warned for using his head as Balthazar became desperate. The Spaniard was still dangerous in the last round, but Benny was too experienced to let this one slip away and the famous referee of the era, Moss Deyong, raised his hand as winner.

Benny's career panned out to the war. There were two wins over Simon Chaves of Venezuela. He won and lost to British bantam champions Johnny King, Johnny McGrory and Johnny Cusick and, in local affairs, he lost a return with Billy Charlton but twice defeated Sunderland's up and coming Tom Smith, whose brother Billy had twice beaten Benny in the Byker man's first couple of years in the sport. Benny served in the RAF during the War and, after his demob, ran a local taxi business.

Mickey McGuire

Although he never reached the championship heights predicted for him after his performances as a teenager, local flyweight Mickey McGuire certainly raised the temperature at the New St James Hall during a seven-month period in 1932. Only just turned nineteen, he out-pointed the current British and European (and, later in the year, World) champion, Jackie Brown, and recorded the then only second knockout win of his career, when he finished the Paris-based world champion, 'Young' Perez. Unfortunately in both cases, to protect the champions' belts, the fights were arranged as non-title.

Born Robert W. Drane in 1913, the Newcastle flyweight followed his father and uncle (Paul McGuire) into boxing. Taking his grandfather's name he became Chuck McGuire, but then changed his handle to Mickey McGuire after a character in a Mickey Rooney film. He started work as a trapper boy in the pit and was even barred from the local bus for allowing mice to escape from his pockets. He completed over fifty fights without defeat before making his paid debut at around the age of sixteen. He had a couple of six-rounders at Bridge End Gym in Byker and made the local press when he out-pointed his fellow novice, Joe Baldersara, at Sunderland. Mick's first manager was Frank Grey, a dole clerk. Later he had to buy himself out of his contract so that he could sign for fruit merchant and leading bookmaker in Newcastle, Jim Gibson. He only lost one from his next thirty-one fights: Bob Francis out-pointing him at the Palais de Danse, Felling on Tyne, in the sixth meeting between the pair, after Mick had won two and drawn three of their previous encounters. The well-matched pair went to a seventh meeting at the Eden Theatre at Bishop Auckland in 1931 and the two lads, who by now knew each other inside out, recorded another draw.

The fight that made McGuire in Newcastle was his scrap for the flyweight championship of the North against the fighter with the 'hard nut' reputation, Ginger Rennie, at the New St James Hall in Newcastle. Mickey liked to come out like a whirlwind for the first round and his busy style served him well in a lot of his big fights. He forced Rennie to rely on defence more than he wanted to. Although the situation changed for a while when Rennie's big right hand found the target in rounds seven and eight, Mick got on top in round eight. Rennie went down in rounds eight and nine and quit in round twelve.

In February 1932, and six wins further down the line (four of them in front of his growing legions of fans at the New St James Hall), McGuire was matched against Manchester's Jackie Brown. Brown's titles were not on the line but the arrangement between the two fighters' managers, Frank Grey and Harry Fleming, of fifteen two-minute rounds instead of the more customary fifteen three-minute rounds was, after the result, to leave a sour taste in Manchester.

Jackie Brown, who had taken part in his first fight in 1925, had only lost two bouts from his last thirty, including a third-round knockout loss, in October 1927, to Bert Kirby, in the rematch for Brown's British flyweight title. Jackie had regained the title in a third meeting a year before he stepped in with the North-East teenager. Brown had followed the British title by clinching the European title against Lucian Popesco (Romania) and had come through two successful defences against Emile Degand (Belgium) and Vincenzo Savo (Italy), all three wins being on points. Boxing writers like Jimmy Butler were making comparisons with the immortal Jimmy Wilde; Butler was even asking his readers to decide who was the better fighter.

Using tactics that he would later employ against 'Young' Perez, Mickey ripped at Brown from the first bell. His two-handed attack saw the champion flying to the ropes. Brown responded with a good right but McGuire not only took it, but he stopped the Manchester man in his tracks with his reply. The crowd was already going wild and Brown knew that he was in for a bruising encounter when McGuire repeated the punishment in round two. Looking badly shaken, Brown was forced to move around the ring, although he did manage to hit McGuire when blows were exchanged. After strong words from his corner in round five, the Newcastle crowd saw the real Brown. But when it looked like he was starting to relent, McGuire came back with his own brand of punching. Both men had their moments, with McGuire having the crowd roaring when his side-step made the champion miss.

Mickey's supreme confidence saw him through the fifteen rounds. Brown did pull himself back into the fight. Despite it not being a title fight, pride was at stake. The champion went for the killer punch in the final rounds, but failed to tag McGuire cleanly. When it did look like Brown might have him in trouble, McGuire was equal to the occasion, backing his man off with a series of first-rate counters. Referee Tom Murphy gave the fight to McGuire. There could not have been any real arguments. Indeed, if Brown had broadcast any, there would have been a riot in the hall. Afterwards Brown told reporters that he would not fight again in Newcastle, even for a purse as large as £50,000. Upset about his reception and the abuse, from what he considered a hostile crowd, Jackie disclosed a fear that the result might go against him in his pursuit of a title clash with world champion 'Young' Perez. In Brown's mind his manager Harry Fleming had played a part in his defeat. Jackie had not boxed two-minute rounds

Mickey McGuire, the 'Geordie' flyweight who beat two world champions but never contested a British title.

for five years. The shorter duration suited his opponent's bustling style. While paying his respects to McGuire, Brown thought his own punching was cleaner and sharper. The points that he should have received, in his mind, would have made him the winner.

McGuire had arrived in the big league and, to build on that reputation, the Newcastle youngster's management accepted a fight in Paris, to be held a month after his Brown victory. Three years older than Mickey, the Frenchman, Valentin Angelmann, had gone fifteen rounds with the American, Frankie Genaro, for the NBA and IBU world flyweight championships, titles that Genaro lost in two rounds in Paris in October 1931 to 'Young' Perez. McGuire did not enjoy his first flight: he suffered with travel sickness throughout the journey. In the fight itself Mickey did well early on and put the Frenchman down for a six count. Angelmann possessed a hefty punch though and he gradually wore his man down. Unfortunately, Mickey was forced to quit in round eight. Angelmann and McGuire would later cross swords another three times in Newcastle. For his next big-name opponent the New St James Hall promoter, John Paget, secured Angelmann's big rival in France, Victor 'Young' Perez.

The fight was arranged at 8 stone 2 pounds, strictly to protect the world champion's crown, although McGuire did not have any real claim to fight for the title. This was a period when, with almost no exception, world title fights were strictly for British champions. In between his two fights with the Frenchmen,

12 September 1932. From left to right: Nick Cavalli (manager), Mickey McGuire, 'Young' Perez, J.J. Paget (promoter).

Mickey completed four wins at the St James Hall. There was one setback: at an ill-fated open-air promotion at the rugby ground in Whitley Bay. The John Paget promotion was a financial flop and Mickey, who was in agony from round four, was still leading on points against Teddy Rollins, when he was forced to retire with a dislocated shoulder. Thankfully the injury had no repercussions for his fight with Perez pencilled in for the month after.

Born in Tunisia in 1911, Perez's career had kicked off at the Central Sporting Club in Paris. He had hammered Angelmann to become the French flyweight champion and had experience in England, two years earlier, when he took Angelmann's place in a fight that had been arranged with Johnny King in Manchester and where he recorded a creditable draw. A further British appearance had seen Perez fortunate to get a decision over Len Benyon at the Royal Albert Hall. When the fight started, McGuire sprang from his corner and crowded the champion, who struggled to cope with the teenager's left-handed hooks and jabs. Mickey easily won the round and, with his band of fervent fans already on the edge of their seats, he finished the world champion only thirty seconds into round two. Sizing his opponent up, the Newcastle hero delivered a perfect left hook, which landed full on the world champion's chin and produced a sensational knockout. Although he had stopped half a dozen opponents, amazingly it was only his second achieved knockout win and it was against a world champion. Paget made overtures about the possibility of a world title fight, but Perez's handlers were only interested in a fight at 8 stone 2 pounds.

Returning to St James Hall to defeat Walter Lemmon and Jim Maharg, for his first fight of 1933, McGuire was matched with Ginger Foran, in an eliminator for Brown's title. The fight went the distance and proved a classic. Mickey was always in the fight and attacked at every opportunity. Foran put him down in round twelve, McGuire was up immediately and straight back in the action. The knockdown helped edge it for Foran: the following day's headline ran 'Mickey McGuire beaten at his own game'. Another points win over Jim Maharg was followed by two twelve-round wins over former British champion Bert Kirby, the man from whom Brown had first won, then lost his titles to, before winning the rubber match.

Brown had badgered his handlers for a return with McGuire. It was a slate he wanted to wipe clean. With Brown refusing to fight in the North East, the Manchester flyweight was ecstatic when the grudge fight was arranged for his own backyard at Belle Vue. The papers built up the fight, with side stakes of £500 offered. Since their last meeting, Brown had repeated a points victory over Emile Degand, in a non-title affair, retained his two titles against Scotland's Jim Maharg on a disqualification and, on 31 October 1932, he had retired 'Young' Perez in thirteen rounds at Belle Vue, to take his tally of belts to three. The new world champion then ended the year with another victory over Degand, this time in Belgium, but, in 1933, Brown's early form had been patchy. He had lost a controversial points decision in Paris. Jackie admitted that he had boxed badly, but not as badly as the French judges seemed to think, when they gave him only three rounds against his opponent, Etienne Mura, who was not in his class. Referee Benny Green disqualified him when he made his first appearance in Manchester as champion. Brown redeemed himself by retaining his world and European titles against Valentin Angelmann at the Olympia and out-pointed Perez in a non-title fight only three weeks before his rematch with Mickey.

Pride was at stake and Jackie Brown was not taking the Newcastle youngster lightly. From early in the fight, Brown's punches had McGuire struggling and the capacity home crowd bellowed for a quick finish. Mickey, bothered by Brown's relentless body blows, sank in round seven, only for referee Tommy Gummer, the former British middleweight champion from South Yorkshire, to rule the punch to be under the belt. It was Jackie's second disqualification in two months and the Manchester idol's followers demonstrated their feelings to the full. Poor Tommy Gummer felt the full wrath. The deafening roar only relented half an hour later with Jackie taking the microphone to appeal to the crowd. A third meeting between Brown and McGuire never took place. While Mickey returned to the North East, to fight almost exclusively in his home town, Brown's next action was a three-title points win over Ginger Foran, the 'Scouser' who had beaten Mickey in an eliminator. Recording a draw with the ever-ready Valentin Angelmann in his next defence, Jackie lost his titles to the ill-fated Benny Lynch, who humbled him in two rounds in front of his Manchester faithful. Brown fought up to the war and, in a career of 140 fights and twenty-four losses, McGuire was one of only three men to beat him twice.

McGuire proved too strong for the European flyweight champion, Praxille Gyde, in a points win at St James Hall and completed his unfinished business with Teddy Rollins, when he knocked him out in round seven at the same venue. Next came three clashes with Valentin Angelmann. Mickey completed his only win over the Frenchman with a disqualification decision and, in the last meeting of their four, a towel was tossed into the ring in round ten of twelve. Still popular in Newcastle, McGuire was stopped in his next major fight against the France-based Philippine bantam, Jose Mendiola, who himself became a big favourite in the North East. When Glaswegian Bobby Magee, another popular boxer in Newcastle, stopped him in his next engagement, it was obvious that at only twenty-one, McGuire's big league days were behind him.

Benny Lynch beat him in four rounds in August 1937 and, in his last recorded fight in 1939, old rival Teddy Rollins of North Shields, who had taken the disqualification result over him seven years earlier, out-pointed him at the Albion Stadium in North Shields.

Billy Charlton

There is no bigger sporting name in the North East than Charlton. There cannot be many who have not heard of Bobby and Jackie and, back in the thirties, Gateshead had its own punching hero in 'Young Charla', the nickname of popular featherweight Billy Charlton. When world champion Freddie Miller had an almost permanent residency in England, and was only beaten once in thirty-one fights (and that by disqualification), the man who should have been given a decision against him was Billy Charlton. There must have been no doubt in the ring great's mind, for he was reputed to have made an agreement for the fight to be excluded from his record, in the famous *Ring Record* book. Scant justice for Billy, but at least some recognition from Miller, who was already leaving the ring, when he was brought back to be announced the winner.

Billy was actually christened John, but took his boxing name from his father Billy, who had been a professional sprinter. It had had been young Charlton's dream to follow in his father's footsteps, but the boxing encouragement came from an interested uncle. Billy threw his first punch at St Mary's Boys Club in Gateshead, before moving on to box at the YMCA, and eventually came under the eye of mentor George Bibby. The then sixteen-year-old had gone to Blaydon to watch Bibby, when a vacancy on the bill saw him step in for his ring debut against Billy Warwick who was half a stone heavier and five years older. Warwick's experience won the day in the four-rounder, but, three years later, Charlton had reversed the decision.

Boxing as 'Young Charla', the abundance of venues in the North East meant plenty of work, although when he fought out of Gateshead, he discovered referees often leaned – sometimes quite heavily – towards the local favourite. The move up to ten rounds came at Carlisle. Peter Miller, a Gateshead fighter Charlton looked up to, was topping the bill. A non-arrival saw the promoter switch opponents and Billy fought Jimmy Maxwell. Recalling the occasion, Billy, well known for speaking his mind, said: 'I lost the decision, but it was such a good fight that his brother, who promoted the fight, said I could go back the following week and fight him again. I did and I lost that one too, but I definitely think I won the two fights.' Billy did beat Maxwell, years later, out-pointing him in Newcastle.

He had twenty-seven fights during 1933, recording twenty-one wins, three draws and three defeats. It was form that made him a regular and popular performer at the New St James Hall and, with the North East being a hotbed of fistic talent during the thirties, there were some good matches to be made with fighters from the neighbouring towns. One of his three defeats in 1933 was against Middlesbrough's Harry Craster, when Billy conceded half a stone. During the next year, he met the up-and-coming Ginger Roberts from Whitley Bay and Benny Sharkey, a massive favourite in Newcastle after his win over the British and former world bantam title claimant Teddy Baldock.

Promoter John Paget persuaded Billy, who was not fully fit, to tackle Roberts, who had already sparred with the Gateshead ringman. Ginger caught Billy with his head, splitting his eye as he put him down. Billy got up to out-point an opponent who would go on to make 150 ring appearances and never be knocked down. By the time he met Benny Sharkey, the Newcastle hero had clocked up nearly a hundred fights. For their 1934 meeting, Billy came in for the indisposed Jim Hurst from Blaydon. Benny threw the heavier punches, although in some cases Charlton was so elusive that a lot of the punches were off target. When he did well, the still teenaged Charlton seemed too overawed to follow through. Experience, particularly in the last three rounds, settled Billy's fate. Benny was a clear winner, but he never looked like putting Charlton down.

Billy came down from 9 stone to 8 stone 5½ pounds to fight 'Nipper' Hampson, the Yorkshire fighter, whose career became dogged by disqualifications. There was talk of Billy meeting the champion, Johnny King, if he came through the fight with Hampson. It was too big a jump though and the Batley bantam knocked him out in round eight.

In the spring of 1935, 'Seaman' Tommy Watson, who had lost his British featherweight title to Nel Tarleton the previous year and was now campaigning as a lightweight, asked Young Charlton to help him prepare for an eliminator for the British lightweight crown. It was a good move for Charlton: Watson had boxed at world title level in New York and not only did the former champion take Billy under his wing, there was a guarantee of some appearances on the undercards of Tommy's fights. One such was Billy's debut at Liverpool Stadium, against Jack Collins, who finished him in two rounds. There was a lot of interest in a rematch with Ginger Roberts and Tommy Watson was in Billy's corner for the big money match. It was a cracking fight. Whichever way the fight went, the result was always going to be unpopular in one quarter. Billy repeated his earlier victory on points.

Londoner Dick Corbett, who twice won the British and British Empire titles in matches with Johnny King and then relinquished them because of weight difficulties in December 1934, travelled north to meet Charlton at the New St James Hall in 1936. Watson had beaten him in 1935 and, after an extensive training schedule under Tommy, Billy was confident that this was the fight to

Billy Charlton, the Gateshead hero well-remembered for his three fights with world champion, Freddie Miller.

propel him into the big league. Corbett, who had beaten Benny Sharkey twice in the last year, did not impress. He held when he could and boxed negatively to many of Billy's moves. Charlton showed his variety and aggression, but it was the former champion who took the verdict. There was a lesson to be learned, and when Billy met Corbett the following year, the decision was reversed.

Early in 1936, Charlton signed a three-year contract with promoter/manager Joe Shepherd. Tommy was not pleased, but public opinion was that Watson's interest had dwindled once his own career was virtually over. One of the first fights was against the Welshman Ronnie James. Charlton was decked in round one. It was not until the end of the fight that it was realised that the Welshman's punch had broken Billy's jaw. Charlton had fought through the pain barrier to beat James on points. Ronnie had not lost many fights and, indeed, on his retirement in 1947, he had only lost sixteen out of 119. In 1944 Jack Solomons brought world lightweight champion Ike Williams to Cardiff to fight James. Williams was of exceptional class and he knocked Ronnie out in round nine.

Billy did not lose a fight under Joe Shepherd until March 1937, when Londoner Benny Caplan beat him over ten rounds in a fight with similarities to his Corbett defeat. Johnny King and Jackie Brown were no longer the only big names in Manchester. Johnny Cusick had emerged to challenge their dominance and Billy's form earned him a chance with Cusick at Belle Vue for the vacant Northern Area featherweight title in September 1937. It was another occasion when Billy thought he was the victim of a hometown decision. Cusick won the title, but it was controversial and ended up in court, with referee Jack Dare successfully suing for libel. Two months later, in a British title eliminator, Cusick won a points decision against Jim 'Spider' Webb in Belfast (Johnny McGrory had forfeited the title), but lost the second eliminator to Benny Caplan (who had beaten Frank McCudden in his eliminator) in Leeds. Kelly beat Caplan for the vacant title and, in the Irishman's first defence, Cusick repeated his earlier victory in Belfast, to become British champion in June 1939. Cusick and Charlton met again for the Manchester fighter's area title at the New St James Hall seven months before Cusick became British champion. Billy had a problem with a burst blister on his foot and, later in the fight, with a cut above his left eye. But he did not hold them as excuses and confirmed that on this occasion, the better man on the night beat him.

The fights that Billy is remembered for more than any others came at Liverpool Stadium in the first two months of 1938 against the popular American featherweight, Freddie Miller.

In a career that would last from 1927 until 1940, the German-American southpaw, Freddie Miller, recorded 247 fights with thirty defeats. Miller came to England (NBA version) in 1934, originally to fight Nel Tarleton. He liked the English golf courses so much that he stayed throughout 1934 and halfway into 1935 before returning west. South Africa was another popular haunt and it was after losing his world title to Petey Sarron in Johannesburg in September 1937, that he returned again to England. His first fight back in the country was against Billy Charlton at Liverpool Stadium, where the fans revered Miller after his win over their own legend, Nel Tarleton. Recalling the first fight, in an article for the London ex-boxers magazine in 1980, Charlton related: 'I felt a wee bit apprehensive. I had seen his fights against Tommy Watson and Benny Sharkey.' Another pointer was Billy's lack of experience against southpaws, even in the sparring ring, and there was the continued rumour that Miller had plaster of Paris sprayed on to his gloves before the fight and allowed to harden. Joe Shepherd's orders were to let Miller do all the work, but Billy was too eager for that: 'I thought I would just let pop with my left hand on his nose and see what he does.' Miller's reply was a drive to the stomach and Charlton was down and rolling on his back. Once he had recovered, Billy spent the rest of round one dancing. Still thinking he knew best, he repeated the action at the start of round two and again he went down from Miller's blow to the solar plexus. The same thing happened in round three. Charlton's recovery was quicker and, though it happened again, Billy was finally able to counter the unorthodox punch by dropping his right elbow. Having found Miller out, Charlton had much the better of the fight; Joe Shepherd, among others, thought that he had earned a draw. Obviously the four early knockdowns carried some clout in the decision, although there was a body of opinion that thought his performance in the second half of the fight was enough to have levelled it.

Charlton pined for a return. He knew Miller would not put him down again and Shepherd, once the rematch was set for six weeks later, got him a left-handed sparring partner in Jim Berry of South Shields. Billy trained hard, for after the first fight there was renewed interest in the rematch in Liverpool. There was no problem with Freddie Miller about meeting Charlton again; he never shied away from anyone. Billy's tactics were based on the knowledge gained from the first encounter. When Miller came in with the right hand, he ducked under it and tried to land with the best punch in his arsenal, the left hook. After the tenth, Charlton told Shepherd he thought he could knock Miller out. Shepherd told him to listen to the betting – the shout was 'I give anyone nine to one, on 'Charla' to win with the draw thrown in and they can have the world champion'. Shepherd told him to accept it, box clever and not to let Miller through with his left to the solar plexus. At the end of twelve rounds, Miller ran to his corner, draped his gown round his shoulders and proceeded to leave the ring. Referee Jack Smith told him to return and Freddie was amazed to get the verdict. Obviously the verdict was not well received and indeed many thought Smith had reversed his decision. There was a third meeting three months later (in between the second and third fights, Miller, despite over 200 fights clocked up, proved he was not a spent force, by knocking out Tommy Hyams in nine rounds, Johnny Cusick in seven rounds and out-pointing Lou Beynon and Frank McCudden). A throng of 10,000 attended a June open-air promotion and, once again, Billy gave Miller a real fright, but could not prevent the experienced American from completing his hat trick of wins against him. Charlton did well early on, but when Miller edged in front, he looked confident enough to win. Billy gave everything in front of his home crowd, especially in round twelve, when he drove Miller all around the ring and nearly out of it. Billy admitted Miller was the better man, while the former champion stated that no English boxer, and he had fought them all, had given him so much trouble. Freddie completed three more wins in England, against Ronnie James, Jack Carrick and Johnny King, before returning Stateside. He retired after his last fight in 1940, aged twenty-nine.

The third defeat by Miller was actually Billy's fifth defeat on the trot, for he had also lost to 'Spider' Kelly and British featherweight champion, Johnny McGrory. The points loss against the Scot, McGrory, in a non-title fight was particularly unlucky and unpopular with the onlookers. It was not all defeats, however; four years since their last meeting, Billy fought Benny Sharkey. Poor Benny was well past his best and, after two counts, Charlton finished him in round six. London had become a city where Billy began to work regularly. He beat Benny Caplan there and his only defeat in the capital came at the hands of 'Spider' Kelly. Ten rounds of non-stop action saw a five-minute standing ovation for both men. Kelly edged his second win over the Gateshead man.

Another well-recalled Charlton fight, although it did not happen in the North East, was his fight with Liverpool legend, Nel Tarleton, in 1939. Tarleton had fought Freddie Miller twice for his world title at Anfield and had lost his British featherweight title to Johnny McGrory in 1936. His educated left tied poor Billy in knots. Halfway through the third round, the fight came to an end. Billy moved Tarleton's left aside and threw a right to his solar plexus. Tarleton went down but, after a foul was called, Charlton was disqualified. Billy had noticed Nel winking to his corner and the North-Easterner came to the conclusion that he had been conned. Joe Shepherd lodged an appeal. Officials at ringside had seen the wink and, as a result, instead of receiving no money as per the rule in a disqualification, Billy got his full money and expenses. Obviously the fight result could not be changed but there was never a rematch between the pair. Tarleton won his title back the following year and kept it until 1947.

Fights began to come by less often, as Billy, with the World War on, had become a private in the army. He did get the chance to meet another thirties legend, Johnny King, in his own backyard at Belle Vue. 'Kingie', still British bantam champion, a title he had held on and off since 1931, had fought over 150 career bouts. He floored Billy for an eight count early on, but after that Charlton was all over him. King could not handle the pressure and Charlton took the ten-rounds points decision. There were hopes of fighting Cusick for his British title, but getting time off for training proved difficult. He did meet Sunderland's Tom Smith, in what he hoped would be for the vacant Northern Area title, but Billy could not get down to the weight. The pair fought anyway. It was an old style Newcastle v. Sunderland grudge match. Charlton never boxed better, but Smith pinched it when he finished the stronger. Round thirteen, when Billy was staggering, was thought to be the crucial round.

Fights now became spasmodic. Ironically for the unlucky fighter, it was felt he was on the verge of the big time when his army service virtually ended his career. Billy himself considered that if he had stayed with 'Seaman' Tommy Watson, his career would have gone further. Bright as a button in later life, Billy wrote a popular series about the famous fights from his era in both newspapers and magazines.

Tom Smith

Boxing on both sides of the war, Sunderland's Tom Smith never had the luck to win a British title. Many older fight enthusiasts agree a title would have come his way if war had not interrupted his career. Often rated in the top three or four to come from the North East, Smith was one of the sport's gentlemen, always with concern for his opponent. A dedicated craftsman without the glamour, speed round the ring was one of his assets and his usual ploy was to be in and out with scoring punches and concentrate on his own defensive abilities when the retaliation came.

Born in Sunderland's East End, Tom was the fourth son of Paddy Smith who had fought at the Star Musical in Sans Street. Paddy's sons followed him into the sport and, to accommodate their interest, Smith senior built a gym in the attic of his home. Oldest brother Billy, whose career ran from 1924–1931, was on the verge of a fight for the championship when he was forced to retire at twenty-two after an appendix operation. Billy had a great record and was only beaten six times out of sixty-seven fights and was never knocked out or disqualified. He out-pointed Sunderland-based rival, Duggie Parker, twice and, in three contests with Benny Sharkey, he beat him twice and drew the other. Among the men to beat him were Tom Cowley in 1931 and 'Nipper' Pat Daly, two years earlier.

When Tom, who started off at the St Pats Boys Club, began to follow in the family footsteps, he asked his older brother's help in turning professional. Billy was in the corner for Tom's debut in 1934 and took over the trainer role throughout his younger brother's career. Tom was a dockworker and the job was good in one aspect; he was able to take time off to meet fight obligations. Smith made his pro debut a month short of fifteen years old, when, in August 1934, he out-pointed John Curry of Wheatley Hill at the Royal Stadium in Sunderland over four rounds and for a purse of 7s 6d. Smith signed up with a local builder, Jack Cummings, who managed a few lads as a sideline and ran his headquarters from a converted gym above his workshop.

Inside a year, Smith had progressed to ten-rounders, rattling up an unbeaten run of thirty-seven fights, before Sheffield's Walter Morton proved too clever at an outside promotion at the West Hartlepool Engineers Club. Smith was keen for a rematch and, two months later, was at his best to out-point Morton at the Albion Road Stadium in North Shields, where Tom was a popular performer.

During the next three years, only three fighters (over five tight or debatable fights) beat Tom. Two of the defeats were against Benny Sharkey in 1938. Benny was past his best and it was revenge for the Byker featherweight against the man in Tom's corner because Billy had not lost in his three prior fights with Sharkey. The first clash in front of a full house over ten rounds at Albion Road was edged by Sharkey but, when the pair were matched again three months later at the same venue, there was an upset in the crowd when the referee gave the fight to Sharkey after Smith had looked to have done all the work. The other three defeats in 1937 were at North Shields, where Tom was an almost permanent resident. Bobby Magee out-pointed him twice over twelve rounds and Billy McHugh, who had drawn with Smith in Leeds, also gained a twelve-round verdict.

The venue switched to St James Hall for Tom's first fight of 1939 and Tom, who had never boxed further south of Leeds and was hardly known out of the North East, had his chance to shine against a reigning British champion. During a career that had started back in 1928, Johnny King had already chalked up over 200 fights. The Manchester ringman had first won the British bantam title in 1932 and had unsuccessfully challenged 'Panama' Al Brown for the world title the year after. He had failed in an attempt to hold two British titles when Nel Tarleton out-pointed him at Anfield for Nella's featherweight title. King had appeared in Newcastle on two other occasions, in 1936 and 1937, when he had won and lost to Benny Sharkey. It was a big ordeal for the twenty-year-old, meeting a champion of King's pedigree who, despite his long career, was still in the top flight at the age of twenty-seven.

Appearing nervous, hesitant and in awe fighting a champion of King's stature, Tom let the older man take the initiative. Smith had to rely on his defence to get him through the early rounds, until King was short with a left lead. The Sunderland lad was in like a flash and troubled the champion with a right to the jaw. It was a confidence gainer and from that round Smith was a different fighter. For everything King tried, Tom had the answer and, if he had been behind in the early rounds, he was in front as the last round beckoned. King could not pull it out of the fire and it was no surprise when the referee, Fred Eastburn, raised Smith's hand.

The quality of Smith's opponents had suddenly come on in leaps and bounds. Two months later, Jim 'Spider' Kelly, the British featherweight champion, was wheeled in at St James Hall. King forecast that Smith would beat Kelly, whose family would create history when his son won his father's old title in 1955 (a feat later emulated by Jack and Brian London). Kelly had beaten Benny Sharkey, Billy Charlton twice and champions like Nel Tarleton, Dick Corbett and Johnny McGrory and the Irish champion's record was nineteen defeats from 107 fights. The local success against Kelly had been draws by Sharkey and Ginger Roberts, the latter in front of Spider's crowd in Belfast. Kelly whose title was not at stake, the fight being arranged at 9 stone 2 pounds, only arrived in Newcastle a couple

Tom Smith, Sunderland's 'boxing gentleman' who surely would have been a British champion but for the advent of war.

of hours before the fight. In fact, Kelly had some courage in even arriving at all, having buried his two-year-old son, who had died in hospital, the day before the fight. The Newcastle crowd was in for another great treat and Smith matched yet another champion in every department. Referee Jimmy Reid gave the fight as a draw and the consensus of opinion was that if the fight had been over more rounds, Kelly would have won it.

Smith's next action in Newcastle, where he was now the regular bill-topper, was against Joe Martinez, who had his challenge terminated through a round-three disqualification for hitting below the belt. Johnny Cusick, taking over King's mantle in Manchester, had taken Kelly's British and Empire titles and a contract to fight Tom in Newcastle was signed. After his performances against King and Kelly, Smith had hoped to meet the winner of the Kelly *v.* Cusick fight for a chance at the title. The fight was put on hold whilst Cusick went on holiday to the south of France. The news broke that Cusick had agreed to defend his titles against Nel Tarleton and the British Boxing Board stepped in to tell Cusick he must honour his contract with Smith and fight Tarleton later. The fight was fixed at 3 pounds over the featherweight limit. Cusick was forced to pay a forfeit when he came in 2 pounds over that. Smith's followers feared he had taken on one champion too many when Cusick floored the Sunderland man with a left hook in round one. But he was quickly up and, although Cusick took the first three rounds, Smith, who had taken Cusick's big shots well, was still very much in the fight. In round five it was Tom's turn to do the hurting with a right to the jaw. From round seven, Smith was in front and Cusick could not bridge the gap. Both men threw every weapon in their armoury in the last couple of rounds and, although it was close, Cusick acknowledged that the better man had beaten him on the night.

While Cusick went on to lose his title to Nel Tarleton in February 1940, Tom finished his best year in the sport with wins over the British Guyana boxer who was resident in England, 'Kid' Tanner and the Welsh champion, Len Beynon. To everyone in the North, Smith's performances during 1939 had earned him a crack at a British title. The British Boxing Board decided otherwise though and ruled that he would have to come through the elimination process. His first opponent was another local lad in the peak of his career – Billy Charlton. Both Billy and Tom had joined the army, Smith joining the Durham Light Infantry, where he reached the rank of sergeant and Charlton the Royal Army Ordinance Corps. It was now becoming difficult to arrange regular fights and it was even harder to get the time off to do the necessary training. The North-East man arranged the fight for the day after Boxing Day. Poor Billy was well over the agreed weight only a couple of days before the fight. He managed to come down half a stone, but could not make the deadline and was forced to forfeit. There had been great interest in the fight in Newcastle, particularly as it was at a time of few promotions, so it went ahead anyway over the fifteen-round championship distance, but not as an eliminator or Northern Area title fight. It proved one of the greatest fights seen in Newcastle.

Despite Charlton's lack of training and weakness from weight loss, he gave what Smith considered to be the hardest fight of his career. Smith won, but there were many who thought that Charlton deserved the verdict. The next stage of the elimination process saw Tom beat Frank Parkes of Beeston, Nottingham, for the Northern Area title. Smith finished the stronger in the last five of the fifteen rounds to take the title. He was not as impressive as in some of his earlier fights, but his performance in the fight's last third made him a clear winner.

After a win in London over the 'Southall Express', Jackie Rankin, Smith went to France with his infantry where he was one of 200,000 Allied troops evacuated from the Dunkirk beaches. With a German invasion expected all sporting activities were cancelled. Finally, after being out of the ring for eight months, Sergeant Smith got his wishes when the Boxing Board announced his fight with Nel Tarleton for both of the Liverpool legend's featherweight titles (British and British Empire). Tarleton rarely defended titles away from Liverpool and Smith, who was under-trained, overweight and surprised that he had been granted a title fight, was allowed two weeks special leave to prepare in Sunderland.

Twelve years older than his opponent, at two months short of thirty-five, the November 1940 fight with Tom Smith was Tarleton's final appearance at Liverpool Stadium. The Saturday afternoon open-air promotion was in the middle of an air raid on Merseyside. Referee Moss Deyong allowed the action to continue and Nella's followers stayed in their seats. As expected, the 'old master' had too much science and ring artistry for his challenger. Perhaps Smith made a mistake by electing to box his man rather than force the pace against his older opponent. Tom's best chance was in round twelve, against an exceptional opponent, whose experience in the ring had started in 1926. Three months later Tarleton came to Newcastle for a non-title fight. Nella was with the RAF in the Orkneys and the chance to return to the ring was welcomed. Smith changed his tactics in the second fight and chased Tarleton all over the ring. Tarleton's defensive qualities were always of the highest order and, although there was never any hint of a stoppage or knockout, Smith ran out a good points winner.

His manager, Jack Cummings, was keen for a return with Tarleton with the titles on the line. Making title fights and having the preparation needed was difficult during wartime and Tom found no real difficulty in taking fights that kept him unbeaten throughout 1941. Glasgow's Don Cameron fell in the first round in Newcastle and in his next fight Smith appeared in the capital. Chances to appear in London had been rare throughout his career but Smith met the Irishman, Johnny Ward, at the Royal Albert Hall, only Tom's second London engagement. Archie Potts, in his excellent and well-researched book *Wearside Champions*, related that Ward, who hailed from Roscommon, was known as a slugger and he weighed in half a stone over the agreed weight. Smith did not want the fight but, to save the promotion from being a disaster, he was pressed to fight Ward at catchweight. Ward's punches were all over the place. He lasted until round three when he left the ring by order of the referee for hitting below the belt. Returning to Newcastle, Smith out-pointed Warren Kendall, stopped Billy Charlton in what would be his Gateshead rival's penultimate fight and completed a second win over the Southern Area champion, Jackie Rankin. For his last fight of 1941, Smith was matched in another eliminator against Dundee's Jim Brady in Leeds. Brady, the British Empire Bantam champion, was now electing to fight as a featherweight. There was a lot of money favouring Brady, but Smith was up to the test. Down in round seven for a nine count and suffering a cut eye from the fourth, Brady was out-pointed in a result that confirmed the Sunderland hero as the official contender for Tarleton's titles again.

In 1942, Smith became part of the Army Physical Training Corps and his new position limited his ring appearances to only three fights during the year. He out-pointed yet another former champion in Dave Crowley, the Londoner who had challenged unsuccessfully for Tarleton's crown at Wembley in 1934, before winning the lightweight championship in 1938 and losing it in the same year to Eric Boon. Crowley, thirteen years in the game, had fought for a version of the world title in New York against champion Mike Belloise. Like Tom, the 'Cockney Jimmy Cagney' liked a tussle with a champion and met over thirty in his lengthy career. Starved of boxing for a while, the famous St James Hall was packed to the rafters. Crowley caused problems early, but Smith ironed out his own errors and finished strongly enough in the last two rounds to take the referee's nod.

A third win over Jackie Rankin, this time at the Queensberry Club in London, took Tom's winning run to ten fights before he had his first setback since the loss to Tarleton two years earlier. On reflection, meeting Ronnie James, who was a full-blown lightweight champion, was an unwise decision. The Welshman's heavy punching proved too much for Smith and, for the only time in the Sunderland man's career, he was beaten inside the distance. James was the number one challenger for Eric Boon's lightweight title, but did not get his chance until 1944. Army commitments curtailed Smith's appearances: in 1943 and 1944 he only fought in army competitions and Tom became the army's lightweight champion in 1944 when he out-pointed Gunner Malone in Blackpool over three rounds.

Sport was booming in the immediate post-war years and, after resuming his career at White Hart Lane where he out-pointed Dave Crowley on the Jack London versus Bruce Woodcock British heavyweight title fight undercard in 1945, Smith had a good audience for his return to Sunderland. Training regularly again and feeling more comfortable at featherweight, Smith repeated his win of six years earlier over 'Kid' Tanner, to the delight of a good-sized crowd at Roker Park. While there was still uncertainty over whether Tarleton would defend his title, Tom proved he was still the logical contender with wins over Benny Duffy at South Shields Greyhound Stadium and Ronnie Clayton, who would become one of the most respected featherweights champions in British ring history, in Leeds. Clayton, who would win the title the following year, would hold the title for seven years and win two outright Lonsdale Belts.

Smith considered his greatest performance to be against Ray Famechon, one of the boxing brothers from northern France. Famechon had turned professional after an unbeaten amateur record of 125 fights in 1944. Smith was the first British boxer to beat him, a feat he achieved over eight rounds at the Royal Albert Hall. Famechon fought for the European title the next year, losing to Al Phillips, but within another year had out-pointed Phillips' conqueror, Ronnie Clayton, at Nottingham, for the crown. The Frenchman also fought Willie Pep for the world crown. Smith was in the ring a week later and dropped a decision to future British welterweight champion Cliff Curvis at Harringay.

Tarleton's long reign eventually ended in 1947, when he relinquished his title on retirement. Rightly, Tom Smith was included in the elimination series. He was due to fight the winner of Joe Carter and Ronnie Clayton, with the winner of that to meet Al Phillips – the last man to fight Tarleton for the title. Clayton was due to fight Smith, with Roker Park touted as the venue, when Smith ruled himself out by stating he could no longer make the featherweight limit. Campaigning as a lightweight, his first fight was against Andre Famechon, whose son Johnny would win a world title for the famous boxing family. Famechon put in a grandstand finish to win the fight. Jack Cummings had his man pencilled in with future fights against the likes of Billy Thompson and Stan Hawthorne, but Smith decided the Famechon fight was his last and announced his retirement at twenty-nine.

The Sunderland hero kept his interest in boxing in the North East and was later a popular president of the former boxers association in his hometown. He died in 1990 aged seventy-one. Smith's record against an array of champions past, present and future, during the war years, proved his ability at the top and many pundits would agree that, if Hitler had not invaded Poland at a time when Tom was at his peak, British title honours would have come his way.

Jack London

Overtaken in lasting fame by his son Brian, who won his father's old title and then went on to challenge Floyd Patterson and Muhammad Ali for the richest prize in the sport, Jack London was heavyweight champion of Britain at a time when winning the title meant something in the game.

Unlucky to be boxing at his peak during the war, when media coverage in sport was at a minimum, Jack London is best remembered by most boxing enthusiasts for the tussle in the ring after his son's fight with Dick Richardson. Prematurely bald, and with a style labelled by some critics as crude and cumbersome, Jack did not boast the glamour of Len Harvey, Freddie Mills or Bruce Woodcock. Noted as a man of few words London liked to do his talking in the ring.

There was a lot of inconsistency in his early fights (understandable when bouts were taken at short notice against much more experienced opponents) when he won only thirty-seven of his first sixty-seven contests. In his first year in the sport, in 1931, he recorded only three wins out of twelve matches and from the summer of 1933 to October 1934, when his class of opponent had stepped up, he only won five out of eighteen. But, when you consider that the youngster was fighting the likes of Jack Casey, George Slack, Charlie Smith, Ben Foord, Gipsy Daniels, Len Johnson and Larry Gains, his fight record of that period is not that surprising. Up to his retirement in 1949, the Hartlepool heavyweight had won fifty-eight of his last seventy-four fights and, before 1935 was out, he had already avenged the defeats of Casey, Slack and Smith.

Born John George Harper in Stanton, West Hartlepool in 1913, the fighting name of Jack London came from the famous author of *Call of the Wild*, who also covered fights for the American boxing magazines that worked their way over to this country. London had already had tryouts in bare-knuckle scraps against local pit lads when he donned the gloves for his pro debut, in January 1931, at a converted factory in Redworth Street. Six feet tall and big framed, Jack was a last minute replacement and finished off the much more experienced but lighter opponent, Barney Stockton, in round one. He was married in the same year that he made his pro debut and boxing helped supplement his job as a lorry driver. With venues available in all the neighbouring North-East cities, London took all the fights he could. In October 1932, he made his first appearance outside the North when he appeared at 'The Ring' in Blackfriars. The promoters at the famous London venue were touting Jack O'Malley, an Australian heavyweight, as a future drawing card. Jack had him down in the first round and, after the pair had happily slugged it out for the punters, Jack was forced to stop with a damaged right hand.

During 1933, London, recently turned twenty, topped the bill at the Crystal Palace against Ben Foord, the London-based South African, who would take the British Empire heavyweight title from Jack Peterson in 1936 and lose the title to Tommy Farr seven months later. Jack's style posed Foord difficulties and, despite him losing a tight points affair, the promoter, Sydney Hulls, was impressed and offered London more outings. London made seven more appearances at the Palace gaining five wins and became a firm favourite at the venue before it was destroyed by fire. Meeting the British Empire champion, Larry Gains, for his last fight of 1933 was a step too far. Jack received his first three-figure packet at the New St James Hall, but was destroyed by the resilient Canadian, who administered London's first knockout, in round two.

After only two wins in his first ten matches of 1934, London finished the year with four wins in the capital. Establishing himself in the top half of the British heavyweight ratings, there were only three defeats in 1935 and 1936. Alex Bell, whom he had twice beaten in London, gained a disqualification win in a third meeting in Edinburgh and Ben Foord repeated his earlier points win over twelve rounds in Plymouth. Former world light-heavyweight champion Tommy Loughran, who had challenged Primo Carnera for his world heavyweight crown in 1934, was in England during 1936 and Jack got his chance against Loughran at Bristol. Loughran was in a different class and the American had the disposition to make the Hartlepool heavyweight seem to be a 'plodder'. Despite the differences, London stuck at the task and made Loughran earn his inevitable points win.

It was a good experience mixing with Loughran and Jack showed his mettle against another of promoter Jeff Dickson's American imports, Obie Walker. It was Walker's fourth fight in England. Back in 1933, he had beaten George Godfrey to claim the title Coloured Heavyweight Champion of the World but had lost the unofficial world title to Larry Gains in Leicester before his fight with Jack. In his other fights, Walker had out-pointed the South African, Don McCorkindale, and beaten the New Zealander, Maurice Strickland. Jack had out-pointed Strickland in Belfast in his fight prior to meeting Loughran. Walker was out-pointed and Jack's success saw him fighting in Berlin in the autumn of 1936.

Following the success of Max Schmeling, the Rhineland had produced an array of good heavyweights, of whom Hans Schonrath was one of the latest. London won over the crowd of 16,000 when his German opponent threw a low punch in round four. The punch guaranteed an instant disqualification, but Jack insisted that the fight continue after he had been allowed two minutes to recover. London won the plaudits of an appreciative German crowd for his win and

Jack London.

afterwards received a medallion for his efforts from the hands of Adolph Hitler. A fortnight later he himself felt the wrath of journalists when the referee stopped his rematch with Larry Gains after eight rounds, because of a lack of action.

London was keen to get a chance with the new British heavyweight champion Tommy Farr, but the Welshman was looking for bigger fish to fry. While he marked time, London's most notable contest was against Buddy Baer, the lesser-known brother of former World Champion, Max. Two years earlier, Baer, aged only twenty (the fight was a six-rounder because of Baer's age), had finished the Irish heavyweight, Jack Doyle, in the first round at Madison Square Gardens. Baer's fight with Jack at Swansea saw the British heavyweight contender collect £400 – his biggest purse so far. In his only other fight in England, Buddy had beaten Jim Wilde in four rounds at Harringay. Like his brother, the 6ft 7in, 17-stone American was a 'banger'. Jack went down a few times, but had got back into the fight near the end of the scheduled ten rounds. The opinion was that, if the fight had been over a longer duration, Jack would have beaten the American visitor. Like Maxie, Buddy got his chance at the world title. In fact, he got two shots at it. In the first meeting against the champion, Joe Louis, the fight terminated in round seven. Buddy's manager had refused to leave the ring and earned Baer a disqualification. The argument was that one of the trips to the canvas had been caused by a low punch. Buddy got his second chance a year later, in 1942, and lasted a round. It was his last fight.

Jack London, the balding West Hartlepool heavyweight who finally got his chance to fight for the British title after thirteen years and 122 fights.

In Northern eyes, London was the leading contender for the British title, but when Farr was forced to relinquish after his fight with Louis had earned him some lucrative fights in the United States, London did not even figure in any eliminating series. Len Harvey completed the last leg of championships, from middleweight to heavyweight, and also added the Empire title by defeating Jack's old foe, Larry Gains. While overtures were made for a challenge to Harvey, Tommy Farr was back from America and licking his wounds after a string of defeats against the cream of the United States' heavyweight division. Twice the London *v.* Farr pairing looked on, but failed to materialise. The fight was earmarked for St James Park, in an open-air promotion, and when the plug was pulled on that promotion a prospective fight in Swansea was scratched, because the Welshman, used to big money in America, wanted a bigger slice than the promoters were prepared to offer.

With England at war, London joined the RAF. Being stationed near Blackpool had extra significance as that was where London and family would relocate. Fights were spasmodic. Jack fought five times in 1939 and then only twelve times over the next five years. The only setback of 1938 was a disqualification against the Canadian, Al Delaney, one of Joe Louis' early opponents. Delaney was out-pointed in Manchester later in the year and, in Jack's first fight of 1939, he knocked Delaney out at the Royal Albert Hall. The coloured fighter, Tommy Martin, who suffered the same fate as the earlier, Len Johnson, in not being considered to fight for the British title because of his skin, out-pointed Jack in his next London engagement at Earls Court. Twenty months later, during the course of which Jack had five wins, out-pointing, at the back end of his career, old adversary Larry Gains twice, Martin and London met again in an eliminator capacity.

The Hartlepool-born fighter had completed a decade in the sport and the eliminator against Martin, despite Jack's continuing position as one of his county's leading heavyweights, was his first recognition (back in 1937, he had had a couple of eliminators for the Northern Area title, but had never fought for the championship). Jack was in good form in out-pointing Martin in Manchester and Len Harvey, now approaching his mid thirties, was the man standing in the way of London's first title. Harvey also held titles at light-heavyweight (his world title was only recognised by the British Boxing Board).

Freddie Mills, a light-heavyweight who did not mind campaigning against heavies, was also eyeing a clash with Harvey who, with the war still ongoing, had not fought since his points win over Jock McAvoy in the summer of 1939. Mills was matched with Jack at the Royal Albert Hall in December of 1941 and, in a comparison of opponents, Freddie had lost in his previous fight to Tom Reddington who had lost twice to London while Freddie, earlier in the year, had stopped Tommy Martin in five rounds. The fight was dull; Mills took the decision on points and got to face Harvey first, the following year. Only a shadow of his former self, Harvey's three-year absence from the ring told the story as Mills, the younger by twelve years, took his light-heavyweight titles in two rounds at Tottenham Hotspur's football ground. Harvey never fought again and, with his heavyweight titles now available, Freddie attempted to become a double champion and was matched against Jack for the British and Empire titles. It had taken Jack London thirteen years and 122 fights to earn a title chance, longer than an entire career for a lot of boxers.

The fight between London and Mills took a year to get off the ground. Initially it was arranged for the small club venue in the capital – the Queensberry Club – in September 1943. Jack spoiled that arrangement when he cracked a rib in spar training with Tom Reddington. White Hart Lane, the scene of the Mills *v.* Harvey fight was mooted, then Leicester, before Jack and Freddie finally got it together at Belle Vue, Manchester, in September of the following year.

Despite the fact that he conceded around 3 stone in weight, Mills was installed as the 3-1 favourite. Freddie was already as popular as any boxer in the country, although no one could visualise quite how popular he would become when the war was over, when he was one of the main players in a British sport boom which would see him crowned as world light-heavyweight champion. London was a different proposition from the last encounter and, although the crowd was with Mills from the start, they began to warm to his older, balding and portly opponent. Neither man had an abundance of ring science, but the effort produced by the two gladiators had the big crowd roaring. Freddie was later to admit in his book *Twenty Years*, that he became anxious when Jack took everything he handed out. Mills was in front after five rounds and was still confident going into round ten. With two-thirds of the fight gone, London switched to the body and slowly the pendulum began to swing. London winded his man in round thirteen with a succession of hooks. Mills tried to turn the tide back but London again swallowed up all the lighter man's punches. The general belief was that Mills was still in front going into the last round. London went toe-to-toe in his efforts. He won the round, but was unsure whether it would be enough to land him the title. Mills thought he was champion but, when the referee gave London the verdict, Freddie was the first to congratulate him.

While Jack was able to celebrate with a trip to West Hartlepool to show off the championship belt, the press deliberated over a return with Mills who, despite his excursions into the heavyweight ranks, was still carrying world title aspirations at light-heavyweight. Jack Solomons, the new entrepreneur in British boxing, had the fight pencilled in for the capital, until the war played a hand and Freddie was posted to India. Bruce Woodcock had fought on the undercard of the Mills *v.* London fight and Solomons, despite the Yorkshireman's lack of experience, was keen to put the former ABA light-heavyweight champion in with Jack. Solomons was building his own reputation on the strength of his big promotions in London and the new British champion was able to demand £4,000 for the fight, nearly as much had earned in his thirteen-year fight career.

The fight was fixed for White Hart Lane in July 1945. With Woodcock, eight years younger, only having been a pro since 1942, and having fought most of his twenty fights as a light-heavyweight, and being in his first fifteen-round fight, London was 5-1 on favourite. Both men had a warm-up fight. Woodcock met the Canadian, Cal Rooney, at the Queensberry Club. The experienced Rooney had amassed 150 wins as an amateur and professional and a supposed reputation of never being knocked out. The Yorkshireman finished Rooney in three rounds, only for the referee to deny him a knockout. Jack elected to go home and drum up local support. A packed open-air promotion in Hartlepool saw him stop Ken Shaw in six rounds. Woodcock came in at 13 stone compared with London's 15 stone 5 pounds. Although contemporary reports stated 40,000 were present in the famous football ground, Solomons, in his book *Jack Solomons Tells All*, claimed that the crowd was only 26,479. Jack attempted to upset the pretender in the opening action of round one. Woodcock, much the better mover, was able to evade his rushes and counter accordingly. The busier of the two, Woodcock looked to building an early lead as a sluggish champion tried in vain to get his man to fight at close quarters. His timing poor in the first few rounds, Jack did gain some advantage in round four when he caught Bruce with three successive head shots. Woodcock's jab had him in the lead when, taking a leaf out of the Mills fight, Jack elected to go downstairs with body shots and, as a result, round five was the champion's best round.

He caught Bruce again and the challenger was now sporting a cut lip and a broken nose. London was starting to push his opponent around, but his success in round five was short-lived. Bruce decided to up his aggression and, when Jack dropped his guard after coping with three quick jabs, Bruce came through with a left to the jaw that saw Jack stiffen up and then drop. A short count followed. Then a right cross had the champion in real trouble. Jack went down a third time and was on one knee when counted out. Later, Jack complained that he could not hear the count because of the noise from the crowd. Woodcock was the champion but could not fulfil the dreams of Solomons. Poor Bruce never really coped with the tougher men on the other side of the Atlantic.

In his comeback fight from the title loss, Jack was out-pointed by Jock Porter, in Scotland, and an announcement was made that he was retiring. A failed garage business saw a comeback and there was immediate talk of a rematch with Woodcock. There were stringent efforts made to put the fight on in the North East, but Solomons and Woodcock's manager, Tom Hurst, had different plans for the man who had taken London's titles. London had three fights in 1946, all of them out of the country. He was beaten in Stockholm by Olle Tandberg, but won his two fights in South Africa against Nick Walmaraus and Joe Foord. During 1947, a chance to get back in the limelight came to nothing when Ken Shaw out-pointed London in an eliminator for Woodcock's titles. After inactivity during 1948, when he even considered an offer to become a professional wrestler, Jack was back fighting in the North East. Three successive wins at Hartlepool were followed by a stoppage defeat by Vern Escoe, a coloured Canadian fighter, in an Empire eliminator at the town's Greyhound Stadium. Jack's last fight was in November 1949 at Earls Court where former US Marine, Aaron Wilson, embarrassingly beat him in round one. It was time to go.

Retiring to Blackpool, he did wrestle for a while, joining the likes of Jack Doyle, Larry Gains and Eddie Phillips, who tried their hand at the game. A period as a nightclub manager followed before he took an interest in the fight careers of his two sons, John and Brian. There was not a prouder man than Jack, when Brian won his father's old British title, creating history in the process. Brian lost his title to Henry Cooper, before boxing against the wishes of the British Boxing Board of Control. Brian went eleven rounds with Floyd Patterson for the world heavyweight title in Indianapolis in 1959.

The famous fight between Brian and Dick Richardson, which saw Jack in the headlines again, took place at Porthcawl in 1960. An after-round argument, after what had been an ill-tempered affair, saw Jack in the ring and trading punches with Richardson supporters and the entertainment provided in the free-for-all was as good as had been shown in the ring. In 1966 Brian fought Muhammad Ali in London and was embarrassingly beaten in three rounds, putting up a pathetic display. Jack was not there to witness his son's sorrowful display; three years earlier he had died of a heart attack in his sleep.

Teddy Gardner

After making his name in successful open-air promotions featuring Jack London at the Engineers Club (in the grounds of the former shipping magnate Lord Ropner), Hartlepool reporter Walter Hazeltine soon had another top-of-the-bill act to delight the local fans. Like London, Teddy Gardner's fighting progress was affected by the second World War and, again like Jack, Gardner came good in the twilight of his career. While London was a heavyweight, the similarly balding Gardner was at the other end of the weight range and, in the decade after Jack's triumph, Hartlepool had its second British champion when Teddy, after first aspiring to win the title at bantam, became British flyweight champion in 1952.

Teddy was born in Middleton, a village near Hartlepool, in 1921. His father was an avid follower of the sport and, from an early age, Teddy was donning the gloves. The pro debut came at the Engineers Club in May 1938. Teddy Baker, who had fought Ernie Izzard for his British lightweight title in 1925, had opened a gym in the North East and in his early teenage appearances, Teddy boxed under the name of his mentor. Jack Herbert was knocked out in four rounds and, after his initial appearances at the open-air venue, Hazeltine, who had been a promoter since he was twenty-one years old, had seen enough to promote Teddy as his headliner. In his first fourteen fights in the North East, before he played his part in the war effort with the RAF, Teddy was only beaten by Middlesbrough's 'Kid' Rich, who was too experienced, and Paddy Gill.

During 1945, Teddy saw service in India and with only a handful of proper fights over the previous five years, he was able to put together an unbeaten run in the East at the Bangalore Hollywood City Stadium. After his demob, Teddy returned to his native North East eager to resume his ring career. He threw his lot in with manager Joe Allen and made the decision to campaign as a bantam. Unbeaten locally during 1946 and 1947, the Hartlepool small man's first setback came in January of the following year, at the Tower Circus at Blackpool. Gus (real name Gerard) Foran out-pointed him, but Teddy was not convinced that proceedings were correct, for he suspected his Liverpool opponent was a lot heavier than he was supposed to be. His defeat was not popular among the onlookers, who had warmed to Teddy after

Foran had floored him after the two boxers had both slipped down. Gardner had offered a handshake, which was met with a big right.

It was back home for Gardner's next four fights, which all finished in eight-round points wins. Another local favourite, Jackie Horseman, who would win the Northern Area featherweight title in 1951, was his first victim and opponent number three was hoped to be Foran until a hand injury saw the Liverpool man pull out. Teddy out-pointed Eddie 'Bunty' Doran, who came in as a late substitute. The Belfast man was rated in the top six British bantams and Gardner improved on that when he added the name of Jackie Paterson to his winning list. Paterson had won the world flyweight title in 1943 when he had knocked Peter Kane out in one round and he retained the title until March 1948 when he lost to Rinty Monaghan in Belfast. Jackie had only defended his three flyweight titles once in that five-year period and had concentrated more on chasing bantam honours. The Scot had won and lost the European bantam title when he stepped in with Teddy in August 1948 but still held his British and Empire titles at bantam. It was a close decision over the Glaswegian southpaw. Gardner had to show self-belief in round six to survive a count, as the hard punching champion threatened a knockout. A repeat victory in Belfast over Doran saw Gardner close 1948 placed seventh in the *Boxing News* bantam ratings.

Stan Rowan upset the chance of a rematch with Paterson when he out-pointed the champion in Liverpool in March 1949. Rowan came to Hartlepool Greyhound Stadium for non-title action later in the year. The win over Rowan proved more conclusive than his win over Jackie Paterson and the talk was now of bringing Rowan back to the North East with his titles on the line. Teddy got his title fight before 1949, but it was not against Stan Rowan who, after losing his Empire title to Vic Toweel in Johannesburg, relinquished his British title because of weight difficulties. Teddy was matched for the title with Danny O'Sullivan at the Royal Albert Hall in December. O'Sullivan, the twenty-six-year-old who hailed from Kings Cross, had a brother, Dickie, who was rated in the top half dozen flyweights in the country.

A train named 'Cock of the North' carried 350 locals, a good percentage of them miners allowed to finish their shift early, to the capital. Teddy Baker, now in the licensed trade in London, was in Teddy's corner. Gardner did well and certainly did not let his followers down. The chances of a second British title for Hartlepool evaporated with a cut eye at the round-nine stage. Teddy was forced to retire with the injury and it was not just the Hartlepool brigade who thought he was in front on points when the injury occurred. He returned to the ring two months later, cut eyes saw him retire in round four against the Canadian champion, Fernando Gagnon, at the New St James Hall in an Empire title eliminator. There must have been doubts about his future and an eventual manager change and a drop down to flyweight saw Gardner, now approaching thirty years old, have a wonderful couple of years to win titles at European, Empire and British level.

Teddy Gardner, Hartlepool's flyweight king who became a triple champion in the twilight of his career.

Teddy never boxed away from the North East again and, with George Shepherd, the promoter at the New St James Hall, as his new manager, Hartlepool had to share their boxing hero with Newcastle. It made one wonder why Teddy had not boxed at flyweight seriously before, as the Hartlepool small man remained unbeaten throughout the rest of 1950. He tamed the Cuban, Black Pico, and gained revenge over the O'Sullivan family when he out-pointed Danny's brother Dickie, who had already contested the European title on two occasions. The win over O'Sullivan assured Gardner's place in the eliminator stage for the British title. That chance came against the Scot, Vic Herman, at the New St James Hall a year later. Herman, the pre-fight favourite, who had contested the vacant title and lasted over fifteen rounds against Islington's Terry Allen, had support in the Newcastle Hall, but Gardner had too much ability for him. With the crowd behind him, Teddy's left hand did the business and, at the end of twelve rounds, it was the Hartlepool flyweight who had his hand raised by the official. It was Teddy's ninth appearance out of his last ten at the famous Hall where the acknowledged crowd had taken the Hartlepool man to their heart and Gardner's give-everything style had made him an automatic ticket seller. Teddy's other appearance had been at a wind-swept, freezing, open-air promotion at the greyhound stadium in his home town. Promoter Hazeltine had two electric fires in the Moroccan, Charles Bohbot's, corner to try and keep the cold at bay for Gardner's challenger. Bohbot retired eight rounds into the fight.

Promoter Sol Sheckman and Gardner's manager, Joe Shepherd, wanted the fight with Allen at Newcastle and pulled out all the stops to bring the London champion north. The Newcastle party won the purse bid and the fight was set for February 1952. Allen had had a non-title fight a fortnight earlier against a Frenchman, Maurice Sandeyron, and a resulting damaged left eye saw Gardner's title challenge put back a month. To keep his man in shape, Shepherd arranged a return fight with Frenchman Louis Skena, whom Teddy had out-pointed exactly a year earlier. With the European title vacant, championship recognition was sought and obtained (Allen had held the title in 1950 and lost it to the last holder: Belgian Jean Sneyers). Throughout his career, Teddy Gardner had crafted his wins by the points route. Teddy was not one for knockouts. In fact his second ever as a professional had been twelve years earlier. His pleasure was in a battle of skill and science, not to hurt. Even though he had landed a European title in front of his own supporters there was a slight tinge of upset in the Hartlepool flyweight when he knocked the Frenchman out in round three.

Now, after fifteen years as a pro without a title, Teddy Gardner, in the space of a month, had the opportunity to add the British and Empire titles (Teddy had already won an Empire title eliminator back in 1951 against Kaila Persson) to his newly won European belt. His opponent, Terry Allen, had travelled the unusual route of winning a world championship before a British title. Real name Edward Albert Govier, the ambidextrous former Islington barrow boy had won 102 fights from 107 as an amateur. His first big chance had come when Emile Famechon had dropped out of a fight with world champion Rinty Monaghan in 1947. It was a foolhardy decision to fight Monaghan; Allen had not been long out of hospital and was humbled in the non-title fight inside a round. Two years later Allen met Monaghan in his own backyard in Belfast with all four titles on the line (World, European, Empire and British). Terry earned a draw with the Irish legend and, when Rinty hung up his gloves, Allen was matched with Honore Pratesi for the world and European titles. Crowned world champion in April 1950, Terry lost his title to Dado Marino in Honolulu. A year later he had unsuccessfully journeyed to Honolulu again and, by the time he met Teddy, he only held the British title.

Excessive roadwork, to ensure he made the weight, had given Gardner problems with leg stiffness in training and was thought to be the reason for his loss of edge in the early rounds. Allen, who was warned for holding in round three, forced the pace, as he did throughout the fight, but found the Hartlepool man's defensive qualities of the highest order. As the fight reached the two thirds mark, Allen still looked the stronger, although the fight certainly was not going all his way. Gardner responded with steady left jabs, followed by rights to the upper body and when the opportunity arose he found the mark with tasty left hooks. Desperate to keep up the pressure, Allen started to lose accuracy and Gardner, who turned aggressor himself in the final rounds, won points when the action got close. The fight could have gone either way, but to the delight of the home crowd, referee Peter Muir lifted the hand of Teddy Gardner, the new flyweight champion of Britain.

With Terry Allen able to earn world title fights, Shepherd surveyed the possibilities of bringing a world championship fight to the North East. He wired the manager of Dado Marino an offer of £6,500 to fight Teddy for the title in Brough Park. Unfortunately Marino was already earmarked to defend in Japan against Yoshio Shirai. After a return to St James Hall, to out-point Frenchman Maurice Sandeyron over ten rounds in non-title action in a fight in which he endured a canvas trip, Gardner fulfilled an ambition and a promise by defending one of his titles in West Hartlepool. A crowd of 10,000 saw him out-point the Italian, Otello Belardinelli, to retain his European title and overtures were made for Teddy to fight the Japanese boxer, Shirai, who had taken Marino's world title.

Meanwhile it was time for Gardner to make the first defence of his British Empire title. What no one could have predicted was that it would be his last fight. South African Jake Tuli was his challenger in the hall where Teddy had won on his last twelve outings. Tuli, with only eleven professional contests behind him, was vastly inexperienced and what was considered a routine defence turned out to be a nightmare. The twenty-one-year-old gave Gardner the severest hiding of his career with the result that the referee was force to halt the champion after twelve rounds.

No one had to tell Teddy to call time on his career; two days later he had announced his retirement and returned his Lonsdale Belt to the Boxing Board of Control. While Teddy carried on being a full-time publican, instead of a part-time one, it was Terry Allen who made the long journey to Tokyo the following year. Allen lost the fight to Shirai over the fifteen-round distance but, four months later, he regained Teddy's old title. Jake Tuli was not forgotten for a long time in Newcastle. If the young Zulu, who it was rumoured had not shaken hands with a white man until he arrived in England, had not ventured out of South Africa it is possible the North East would not have had to wait until the nineties before it boasted its own world champion.

George Bowes

Completing the trio that included Jack London and Teddy Gardner there came a hard-hitting bantam who extended the prowess of Hartlepool ringmen into the sixties. George Bowes did not emulate Jack and Teddy and bring a title back home but, for a half a dozen years, he was never out of the top three at his weight. There were always going to be comparisons with Teddy and a local writer summed it up exactly, when he said: 'If we could have mixed Gardner's boxing skills with Bowes' punching power we would have produced a champion who would have ruled the world small weights division for years'.

Born in 1936 at Hesledon, near West Hartlepool, there was fighting in the Bowes family's blood, for George's grandfather had been a 'bare knuckler'. Like one or two other Northern boxers, young George was interested enough to go watch friends at a tournament and then try his own hand after a non-arrival. Once bitten by the boxing bug, he joined the Boys Welfare Club in Hartlepool at fifteen. For three years he was Northern Counties ABA champion at flyweight and then bantam. Traditionally round the Durham coalfields, lads followed fathers down the pit and Bowes became coal filler at Blackhall Colliery. Particularly in the sport's earlier days, boxing was often part of the miners' recreation, when pits boasted their own champion and would create rivalry with other pits by challenging their champions. The National Coal Board used its initiative by installing its own championships and, in 1954, George Bowes was the national flyweight champion.

Signing with George Allen, his pro debut came in 1957 at West Hartlepool, where Bowes beat Manchester's Harry Dolan in three rounds. With four straight wins, three of them inside the distance, George made his debut at the famous St James Hall. His opponent was a name instantly recognised by local fighting fans, for Jake Tuli had been the man to retire George Gardner five years earlier. Admittedly the former British Empire flyweight champion was on the comeback trail after a brief retirement, but Bowes had only three months and sixteen rounds of experience as a professional. Tuli had lost his Empire title to Dai Dower and later had unsuccessfully challenged Peter Keenan for the Empire bantam championship. In two comeback fights, the African had tasted two defeats, including one to Irishman Billy Rafferty, the fighter who had gone the distance with George, in the latter's third fight.

Despite the bantam's brief experience, the Hartlepool fight fans, accustomed to top boxers, got behind their latest hero and there was nearly a full house at Newcastle, with special trains and buses bringing supporters from the 'Pool'. Experience counted for nothing, Bowes took command from the opening bell and he had the African reeling with a series of savage blows to both head and body. Tuli returned the punches in round two and Bowes, knowing that this fight was the one to help put himself on the title ladder, was able to respond. Telling combinations put Tuli down in round three and only overeagerness spoiled a stoppage in the round, as the bell saved the former champion. The African was down again in round four and he needed a champion's survival instincts to last the eight rounds, the fight being too one-sided at the end. Local pride had been restored after the Tuli fight. George made his bow in the capital, when he drew with Eric Brett at Harringay on the Brian London v. Willie Pastrano bill. Indian born Brett had taken part in a fight at Doncaster in 1957, in which his opponent Jackie Tiller had died from injuries.

A twelve-fight unbeaten run inside a year saw George race up the British rankings and earn a place in the British title eliminator series against the unbeaten Belfast southpaw Freddie Gilroy. Something had to give and Freddie came in to the lion's den at Hartlepool but took the decision over ten rounds. Within eighteen months, Gilroy had not only taken Peter Keenan's British and British Commonwealth bantam titles in an eleven-round stoppage in Belfast, he had wrapped up the European title with a fifteen-round victory over Piero Rollo.

The Scot Frankie Jones had become British flyweight champion in eleven rounds in July 1957. Forced to fight bantams in between title fights because of a lack of quality 8 stone flyweights, Jones, who had beaten Bowes back in their ABA days en route to the final, could not compete with the hard punching bantam. George put the Gilroy defeat behind him with a stunning first-round knockout. Bowes had become the latest in a long line of crowd heroes at St James Hall and his next five fights were for promoter Joe Shepherd in Newcastle.

A pro since 1951, the Belgian, Pierre Cossemyns, had found mixed fortunes on his previous visits to Britain. He had beaten and lost to Hogan 'Kid' Bassey and lost to Peter Keenan and Freddie Gilroy in four rounds and also recently to former Olympic medallist Terry Spinks. Newcastle United were playing an FA Cup tie on the same night at St James Park, so the wily Shepherd altered the fight time back to 9.15p.m. to accommodate both sets of fans. Bowes nearly blasted the Belgian out in round one before the bell intervened and he repeated the punishment again in round six, but the Belgian did enough in the remaining rounds to earn himself a draw.

Eric Brett had been the man to stop the winning run the previous year in the draw at Harringay. When the two met again, Brett did well in the opening

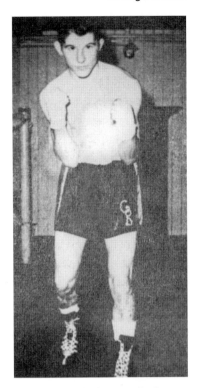

George Bowes continuing the tradition of Hartlepool ringmen. The town's hero in the 1950s and '60s, he contested the bantam title in Belfast.

rounds. Bowes had learnt from the first fight though, and when the opportunity arose, his body punching saw off the Indian-born bantam in round five. Brett stated afterwards that Bowes was the hardest puncher he had ever faced and could see the Hartlepool boxer taking the British title. Not having his original opponent, Shepherd had to rejig the bill after a pullout: the South African champion Graham Van der Walt went in round seven in George's next Newcastle date. The African, who had gone fifteen rounds in an Empire challenge, proved a spoiler until George got to him in the middle rounds. Shepherd pulled off a coup when he brought the current European flyweight champion, Young Martin, to Newcastle. The fight had been on and off due to the Spaniard's illness and there was great interest to see Bowes in against a champion who had put Dai Dower down eleven times in taking his title. The Newcastle fans were in for another short-round victory when a single punch uppercut landed on the end of Martin's chin and brought a round–two knockout. Bowes had blown away both British and European flyweight champions inside two rounds, but was seemingly no nearer to another bantam eliminator. The interest that Terry Spinks was receiving at the same weight in London invoked rumblings of a North–South divide. The Belgian, Cossemyns, who had lost to Spinks again in his previous fight, returned to Newcastle for Bowes's fifth and final Newcastle appearance of 1959. Needing to keep in the eliminator frame, the Cossemyns rematch nearly turned out to be a bigger disaster than it was. Down several times early on, Bowes rallied in a great comeback, but it just was not enough to take the verdict. George's unbeaten run since the Gilroy defeat had ended and worse was to follow. Len 'Luggy' Reece, who had lost to Frankie Jones for the British title, out-pointed him in Luggy's native Wales.

It took George fifteen months, a change of manager and an unbeaten run of ten fights to get back into title contention. Champion-maker George Biddles was the new manager behind the Hartlepool bantam when he challenged the Scot, Billy Rafferty, in Belfast in April 1961 for the right to meet champion Freddie Gilroy. George had beaten Rafferty in a fight early in both fighters' careers.

The return encounter was controversial. Bowes thought he had won the fight, but there was a big talking point over which Biddles made a complaint afterwards. George put Rafferty down near the ropes, and when the Scot came up quickly at the four second count, he held on to the ropes, while the referee, making sure George had gone to his neutral corner, carried on counting for another four seconds. The extra seconds helped Rafferty to recover and keep out of trouble for the rest of the round. The opinion was that in those four seconds, Bowes could have finished his man and the mistake by the referee in continuing the fight cost him the chance. Rafferty, who had lost to Gilroy in thirteen rounds in an attempt for Gilroy's three titles back in 1960, challenged the Belfast man again in March 1962. Gilroy had lost his European title to Pierre Cossemyns and had been out-pointed by Alphonse Halimi for the vacant world title between the two fights. He stopped Billy in one round fewer, in their second meeting, but before the year was out had lost his two remaining titles to Johnny Caldwell.

Including the Rafferty defeat, Bowes lost half of his next fourteen fights. He dropped out of the bantam ratings and began fighting regularly as a featherweight. George fought the unbeaten British champion Howard Winstone over ten rounds and, although he could not stop the Welsh legend from taking his victim tally to thirty-three, Winstone's handlers liked the Hartlepool man enough to invite him for sparring in preparation for future title fights.

George's fading dream of fighting for the title suddenly became a reality when he had another managerial change and signed with Dennie Mancini. But the title shot was not at featherweight, it was at his former weight – bantam – and there was to be no elimination process as he was matched with Johnny Caldwell for the vacant British and British Empire championships. After taking Alphonse Halimi's European version of the title and then successfully defending against the Frenchman, Caldwell had lost to Eder Jofre in San Paolo in a world title unification fight. Later, in 1962, Caldwell had lost the 'Battle of Belfast' against Gilroy and, after Freddie had relinquished, Johnny, the strong favourite to land Gilroy's old titles, met Bowes at the ABC Cinema in Belfast in April 1964.

There might have been arguments as to whether Bowes deserved his title shot, but he certainly proved he was not just there to make up the numbers against the 1-4 favourite. Putting on an exhibition for his fervent fans, Johnny looked comfortable for the first three rounds, but from round four Bowes' punching started to find the mark and upset Caldwell's rhythm. There was still nothing in it when George became bothered by an eye injury. Near the end of round seven, the referee decided the injury had ended George's challenge. Immediately there was an outcry, because the fight had ended only fifteen seconds from the end of the round, not allowing the Hartlepool fighter's corner to work at the cut. The other angle to the controversy was that George believed Caldwell had caused the injury with a head butt. While Caldwell would lose his titles to Alan Rudkin a year later, Bowes had a couple of years in the sport as a featherweight.

When Frankie Taylor, who looked on a sure-fast route to fight champion Howard Winstone, stepped into the ring with the twenty-eight-year-old George Bowes at Newcastle in the autumn of 1964, it was not predicted that the younger boxer's twenty-three fight unbeaten record would end. It was a monumental contest; both men were that type of boxer. When it looked as though George's big shots might be crucial, Taylor pulled it round. During the in-fighting, referee Tommy Watson, the old champion, warned Taylor a couple of times over the use of his head. When Taylor failed to heed the warning, Watson pulled the Lancastrian out and Taylor lost his record on a seventh-round disqualification. Before the year was out, the pair fought again at the Royal Albert Hall and, with Taylor on top in the first half and Bowes on top in the second half, the verdict was a draw. George's next fight saw him return to Newcastle, where the Frenchman, Yves Desmarets, stopped him in ten rounds. In June 1965, with both fighters switching to bantam there was a third meeting with Frankie Taylor. This time Taylor had his measure in an eliminator at the Royal Albert and, after being down twice in round three, George was finished in round six. While Taylor's career came to an early conclusion after a couple of defeats against South Americans, with only three wins out of his last nine fights, George called it a day in 1967.

With the same enthusiasm and endeavour that he had showed as a boxer, whether he was running gyms or looking after top fighters, George never stopped working for the sport in the North East. Although he never won his own title, he is thrilled that some of the boxers with whom he's been heavily involved have.

Maurice Cullen

The classic left jab is an attribute of many great champions and in Durham, during the sixties, they boasted their own exponent of the boxing art. Maurice Cullen's left fist was so educated that one writer likened it to the trombone-playing arm of the American music legend Tommy Dorsey. An outright Lonsdale Belt winner at lightweight, few boxers rivalled the former pit worker's fitness and 100 per cent effort. Not too fashionable outside the North, where audiences would go for a big puncher rather than a craftsman, Cullen's three year title reign would have certainly been greater but for the advent of one of the greats of the weight division, Ken Buchanan.

An apprentice as a pipe fitter at Wheatley Hill Colliery (he later moved to Shotton), there was no one more pleased than his father, Mick, when the seventeen-year-old related he wanted to box in a ring. Mick, who had arrived in the North from Roscommon for work in the Durham pits, had fought in local promotions and loved to earn a bob when the travelling boxing booth hit the area. Trained by former bantam Pat Gorman, success came for Maurice at the National Coal Board championships where he won the featherweight title in 1956 and the lightweight championship three years later. There were many knock downs during the amateur days, but problems with his right hand made him become more reliant on the intelligent left and, as a result, points wins began to feature more in the Cullen record. Another asset in Maurice's makeup, which was to come to light, was that he possessed seemingly limitless stamina, which was found to be attributed to a benevolent heart condition called *bradycardia*, the same reduced heart rate that had helped Henry Armstrong win three world titles before the Second World War.

His brother Terry became his manager and Maurice made a successful professional debut in November 1959, out-pointing Scotsman Ricky McMasters at Farrer Street Stadium in Middlesbrough. It became unlucky thirteen, when Cullen, after twelve straight wins was out-pointed by Jim 'Spike' McCormack, at the National Sporting Club in Piccadilly, in Maurice's second visit to the capital. The decision was not popular and the usually affable club members made their opinions heard over the referee's decision. Five fights later McCormack was out-pointed at Belle Vue and, to kill off any other doubts, Cullen repeated the win, close though it was, over the North of Ireland champion in front of Mo's own crowd at the New St James Hall in the Shotton fighter's first outing of 1962.

One of the fights that helped Cullen get noticed on a wider scale, as he propelled his way up the British lightweight rankings, was his first big top of the bill fight in Newcastle's famous boxing hall. He might have been in his late thirties, but the Algerian-born Frenchman Guy Gracia still had a reputation and some big names had fallen by his wayside. He out-pointed the British champion, Dave Charnley, in the Dartford southpaw's fourteenth professional outing and did it again four years later in 1959, when Charnley was competing on the world stage. Other notables on his record included Darkie Hughes, Joe Lucy and Willie Toweel in Glasgow, a fight the South African later avenged in Cape Town. In seventeen previous appearances in Britain, his only setbacks were against Frank Johnson, twice winner of the British lightweight title in the fifties, and Dagenham's Ron Hinson who beat the Algerian twice. In the early rounds it looked as if Garcia was a spent force as Cullen's left quickly piled up the points. The Frenchman showed the St James Hall crowd that he was not that far over the hill when he figured strongly in the middle rounds of the ten-round fight. Garcia made his opponent work for his win as Cullen's jab assured the points totted up on the right side.

Maurice's form over 1961 and 1962 had made him one of the leading challengers to Dave Charnley, who had been British champion for six years in succession. The other two main fighters in the frame were the Merseyside pair of Dave Coventry and Johnny Cooke. Maurice already held a decision over Cooke in an early fight for both ringmen. Cullen dropped a controversial ten-round decision to the then unbeaten Sammy McSpadden in London, but the result did not affect Maurice's chances in the title stakes. He out-pointed Dave Coventry at Finsbury Park in 1962 (Coventry was beaten by Cooke during the same year for the Central Area title), in a real hard scrap in which Cullen had a closed eye from round three. In his next engagement the Shotton boxer beat Cooke, who had always had the edge in the pair's amateur battles, in a title eliminator over twelve rounds at Liverpool Stadium, to clinch his title fight with Dave Charnley. Prior to his fight with Charnley, Cullen out-pointed another title contender in London in Vic Andretti. Now for Charnley; in some ways, Cullen was not looking forward to it – he did not like fighting southpaws.

The former ABA champion had out-pointed Joe Lucy at Harringay, to become British champion in 1957. South African Willie Toweel had blighted his Empire title hopes soon afterwards, but when the return came nearly two years later, Charnley delighted the Empire Pool crowd by knocking out Toweel in ten rounds. The European title followed, though the European Boxing Union took it back when Charnley failed to defend it within a stipulated period. Charnley twice challenged the American, Joe Brown, for his world title. The first fight,

Maurice Cullen, County Durham's great left-hander whose three-year title-reign would have been longer if not for the arrival of all-time great Ken Buchanan.

in Houston, had ended in a five-round retirement, due to an eye injury to the Dartford southpaw and in the second meeting Charnley had taken Brown all the way. Earlier in the year, Charnley had finally got the better of the ageing Brown (nicknamed 'Old Bones') when he stopped him in six rounds in Manchester. But by then Brown was titleless, losing his crown to the Puerto Rican, Carlos Ortiz, in April 1962. Charnley had not defended his British title for eighteen months, since he had destroyed Darkie Hughes in one round in a three-title fight. Maurice's fight with Charnley, at Belle Vue in May 1963, was just for Charnley's British title, because Bunny Grant had taken his Empire title over fifteen rounds in Kingston, Jamaica.

At the pre-fight press gathering, Mickey Duff, the matcher of fight promoter Harry Levene, revealed that he had arranged terms with Ortiz's manager Bill Daly and that the Puerto Rican would earn £25,000 for defending his title against the winner of Charnley and Cullen. His friendship with Welsh welterweight Brian Curvis, who helped in Cullen's preparation, saw Brian's brother, Cliff, in the Durham man's corner. The press speculated whether Cullen could keep his jabbing style going for fifteen rounds. It was expected that Charnley would catch him up in the later rounds, especially as it was Cullen's first fight at the championship distance.

It was not a spectacular fight and, at the end of the fifteen rounds, it was Cullen who received the biggest ovation, despite referee Billy Jones raising

Maurice interlocks arms with Vic Andretti.

Dave Charnley's hand as the winner. Opinions of the winning margin varied. Some had Charnley winning nine rounds, others had only one point in it and some even had Cullen winning. Charnley had genuinely seemed worried in the final rounds and at times looked desperate to force victory. Though his speed of foot and raised-arm defence caused the champion problems, Cullen was guilty of giving too much respect at the start, when he seemed in awe of Charnley, and dropped short with some of his early jabs, which gave his opponent that early initiative.

Carlos Ortiz did come over in the autumn, but not to fight Dave Charnley. In the final throes of his career, Charnley dabbled with a move up to welterweight. Cullen's mate, Brian Curvis, out-pointed him and, after Emile Griffith had floored him three times in January 1964, it was time to say goodbye to one of the country's best fighters of the fifties. Ortiz, who had beaten Charnley in a non-title fight at Harringay in 1958, was matched in a ten-round non-title fight with Maurice at Wembley. Prior to his visit to the Empire Pool, the Puerto Rican, who had moved to New York as a nine-year-old, had confirmed his position as the best lightweight by becoming undisputed champion (WBA and WBC) by stopping Doug Valiant. Levene's rival Jack Solomons promoted the fight and

Cullen gets underneath Edie Mensah at Wembley, December 1960.

to Cullen it was important to show that he deserved to be in the same ring as a world champion. Maurice certainly did that; Ortiz's forward style was tailor-made for Maurice's left. He took the champion's best shots and his tasty left hooks saw Ortiz leave the ring with bruises and cuts around the eyes. Ortiz, who joked later that 'Cullen was the fastest lightweight in the world over a hundred yards' won the bout on points. It was a crucial last round, when Cullen hit the canvas, which confirmed the victory. Although the result was never in any real doubt, Cullen was not only in the frame for another crack at the British title, his performance against Ortiz had raised hopes of the possibility of a world title fight with the Puerto Rican. A British fighter did gain a decision over Carlos Ortiz, but Maurice Cullen never got another chance. Ken Buchanan brought the curtain down when he stopped Ortiz in the Puerto Rican's last fight in 1972. Before that, Ortiz had lost and regained his title to Ismael Laguna, and finally lost it to Carlos Teo Cruz in 1968.

Cullen returned to Wembley for a second points win over Vic Andretti. The Hoxton lightweight had put himself back into the title ratings with two wins over Sammy McSpadden, who had beaten him twice earlier. A year later Cullen was back in the capital, making his second attempt at a British title. His opponent was Dave Coventry. The hard punching Merseysider, who had been schooled in America and had fought his first six professional contests there, had been scheduled to meet Charnley for the title. Injury had ruled out the pairing and the title fight was rescheduled to take place after Charnley's fight with Emile Griffith. Charnley had already made the Lonsdale Belt his own after the win over Cullen and after the defeat and the way he lost to Griffith, Charnley elected to hang up his gloves on a distinguished career and relinquish the title. It was Coventry's first major fight at Liverpool Stadium since the embarrassment of his one-round defeat at the hands of the American, James J.D. Ellis. (Ellis stopped Cooke in eight rounds, but failed to beat Charnley.) The Merseysider knew all about the piston-rod left, but could not do anything about it. Every round followed a similar pattern. Coventry was forced to chase without finding a real opening. Cullen irritated the Liverpool crowd with his back-pedalling, but the Cullen supporters knew their man was on a winner as 'Blaydon Races' rang out at the final bell. There had never been any real doubt, but Cullen's rally in the last round, when two big crosses had Coventry hanging on, definitely settled the issue. Maurice Cullen was the first British lightweight champion from the North East since Billy Thompson in the forties (although born in the North East, Billy lived and boxed out of Hickleton Main and is generally accepted as a South Yorkshireman).

Maurice's first appearance as champion came in a distance win over 'Joe' Rafiu King at Brighton Metropolitan Club. On paper it was the best result of Cullen's career for King, who had contested a lot of his early fights in France and Italy, had carried a number six in the world ratings. In 1963 King had gone fifteen rounds in Mexico City with Sugar Ramos for the WBC and WBA featherweight title. More recently, King's career had begun to slide and, before his defeat by Cullen, he had lost to Vic Andretti and Howard Winstone. Empire champion Bunny Grant was out-pointed in a non-title fight before the new British champion attempted the next stage towards an outright Lonsdale Belt.

Cullen's first challenger, the fight going ahead at Wolverhampton in 1965, was former opponent Vic Andretti, who the champion had already beaten over eight and ten rounds. Managed by Jim Wicks, Andretti, unbeaten since his second loss to Maurice, eleven fights earlier, had added the names of both King and former world champion Joe Brown to his list of victims. Despite being four years younger, Andretti had contested more fights than the champion and his first title fight was his fiftieth as a professional. As was expected in all Cullen fights, the fight went the distance. Maurice, more incisive than usual, retained his title, although his opponent did not readily accept the result. The challenger, who had found difficulty getting near Cullen, went down on his knees in frustration at the end. Afterwards, he said he felt as if he had won by a mile, even admitting that he had eased up on purpose in rounds thirteen and fourteen because he knew he was in front. Boos and whistles greeted the result and two fans tried to get in the ring to demonstrate their feelings.

During 1966, Maurice participated in a series of fights in Newcastle. The Frenchman, Roger Younsy, only lasted two rounds. Only once before had Cullen taken an opponent out faster. Former champion, Tommy Watson, had been the third man who had brought proceedings to a halt. The French made an issue over his stoppage decision against a fighter who it was reputed had not been down in fifty fights. Watson felt strongly that he had made the right decision and afterwards he resigned his referee post. There was no immediate outstanding challenger for Cullen's title and when it was announced that Maurice's second title defence would be in Newcastle against Birmingham's Terry Edwards, a boxer who had only won half of his twenty-eight fights, the interest was muted. As a result, St James Hall was only half full. Manager George Biddles had been successful at getting the best from bad situations in the past, but Terry Edwards was not to be one of his victories. The press headlines stated that the winning punch, in round five, which clinched the outright Lonsdale Belt, had been from Cullen's right hand and the champion had not won successive fights inside the distance for six years. Promoter, Lawrie Lewis, who had lost money on the event retorted in the papers: 'You can forget me bringing Carlos Ortiz to Newcastle'. Argentine Valeno Nunez became a third short-round victim in Newcastle and then, in January 1967, Cullen's unbeaten run, which was approaching four years in duration, went in London.

The name Lloyd Marshall had upset British boxing in the past. Back in 1947, the unknown American pulled off a shock victory over the British and eventually world light-heavyweight champion. Twenty years later, another American, with the same name, knocked Maurice out before the end of round one, the first time the British champion had failed to go the distance in a professional defeat. Cullen explained to John Jarrett, in the latter's excellent book *Hall of Fame*, that he had suffered with enteritis the week before the fight. Promoter Jack Solomons had put pressure on his brother and manager, Terry, for Maurice to fight, with the ultimatum that his fighter would not compete again in Britain if he pulled out.

Solomons won the purse to promote Cullen's next title defence, in Newcastle. Since his man's defeat in Wolverhampton, Jim Wicks had clamoured to get Andretti a return with Maurice. This time Cullen was fighting a proven name and the knowledgeable Newcastle boxing fraternity turned out accordingly. The two boxers put up a great fight and, at the fourth attempt, Andretti still could not get the better of his rival. Cullen's performance in Wolverhampton and his defeat by Marshall had raised some doubts, but the former Shotton miner, and his left hand in particular, were back to their brilliant best. Andretti could not get near him for long periods. There was a scare near the end, when Cullen was troubled by a cut near the eye. Andretti applied late pressure, but the champion was able to hold on to record probably his finest title victory. Maurice, who worked as a lifeguard during the summer, had never boxed outside of England but in his two remaining fights of 1967, he fought in Helsinki and New York. He out-pointed

Olli Maeki in Finland and repeated the dose to Mike Cruz at the legendary Madison Square Gardens.

Back in his home country after his New York experience, it was time to defend the three-year reign of his lightweight title. Ken Buchanan, with twenty-three straight wins in his three years in the sport was, at twenty-two, the new kid on the block. Most of the canny Scot's appearances had been in members clubs. It was a situation Buchanan never warmed to, but Kenny was unfortunate to be boxing in an era when the public hall venue was not at is height and fighting in front of the dinner jacket brigade was a necessity. Buchanan had earned his right to fight for Maurice's title after an eliminator win at the National Sporting Club against old Cullen rival, Spike McCormack. The fight was at the Anglo Sporting Club in February 1968. Throughout the fight, Buchanan was very much the aggressor and first to the punch, facets which saw Cullen's confidence fade as the rounds went by. In his book *The Tartan Legend*, Kenny talked about his pre-fight advantage: 'I won the weighing up at the weigh in and nobody noticed except me and my opponent. Both of us knew that would give me the edge in the fight'. The younger man's speed troubled Maurice and, as Buchanan came forward, Cullen found himself forced to back-pedal for a lot of the fight. Buchanan's accuracy saw Cullen down several times and, with the champion starting to look tired and hurt, Buchanan went in for the kill in the eleventh round. Blows rained down on Cullen's head and he was forced to sag. The Durham man was up on his feet when the fight finished, but the referee knew the signs. The champion was beaten and did not want to carry on.

Buchanan was destined for greatness and unfortunately for the British boxing fan, particularly in Scotland, Kenny had to fight in America to achieve his world standing. After he became champion, Buchanan only ever boxed once in Scotland, in a title fight with fellow Scot, Jim Watt, in Glasgow. Buchanan lost his unbeaten record in Madrid to Miguel Velazquez in search of the European title. Before 1970 was out, he had won the world lightweight title in San Juan, Puerto Rico, against Ismael Laguna. Defences against Ruben Navarro in Los Angeles and Laguna in a return at Madison Square Garden followed, before the legendary Roberto Duran took his title in New York in fourteen rounds in 1972. After retiring in 1975 he found himself short of money and made a comeback in 1979. The nine-fight comeback sadly ended in four defeats, the last against the Hartlepool ringman, George Feeney, who could not really claim restoration of local pride because, by 1982, Kenny Buchanan was only a shell of his former self.

After his defeat by Buchanan, his sixth loss out of thirty-eight, fighting light-welters and full-blown welters, Cullen had two more years in the sport before retiring in January 1970. Throughout his professional career, Cullen had not lost successive fights. But the Durham boxer was on a hiding to nothing going over to South America to box the Brazilian Joao Henrique, who was unbeaten in twenty-one fights, and who never fought outside Sao Paulo. Henrique's unbeaten record went up another notch and two years later the Brazilian made an unsuccessful attempt at the WBC light-welterweight title. There were successive appearances in Copenhagen, where Cullen out-pointed Borge Krogh and lost to the popular American, Eddie Perkins, who had boxed all over the world and who, at one stage, had held the world junior welterweight title. In his penultimate fight, Maurice ended the unbeaten run of Coventry welterweight Bobby Arthur. Bobby only won two out of his next eight fights, but did gain a disqualification result over John H. Stracey, to take the British welterweight title, a title he lost to Stracey in four rounds in the return. Cullen's last fight was a points win over Victor Paul at Solihull, the scene of his last three fights.

John Jarrett, who has covered the North East in the British boxing bible, *Boxing News*, for many years and saw many of his local fights, labelled him one of boxing's most modest talents and certainly one of this country's most underrated champions. Maurice kept in touch with the local scene and attended a boxing dinner shortly before he died, aged sixty-three, in November 2001.

John Feeney

Some members of the fighting fraternity have expressed the notion that, if it had not been for the tragic death of British champion Johnny Owen, Hartlepool's John Feeney would not have achieved any success outside of the North East. It is an unfair criticism, for it is more than likely that Owen would have given up his domestic title in search of more world title fights. Another fact is that, had the super-bantamweight division been around in the first half of the eighties, John Feeney would have carried titles for the majority of his career. For Feeney was always more comfortable at around 8 stone, 10 pounds, often having to lose weight for big fights during his days as a bantam. 'Fighting Man of the North' is an apt description of John Feeney. Always an aggressive fighter, Feeney gave his all in fights, often fighting in his opponent's backyard and, apart from a disqualification, the Hartlepool hardman was only stopped once in forty-four fights.

Born in May 1958, the year after his brother George, young Feeney was a graduate from the Hartlepool Boys Welfare Club. Junior ABA champion in 1974, the Hartlepool youngster gained Young England representative honours and became runner up in the ABA bantam senior competition in 1976. Another one of Hartlepool's favourite sons who had competed at the same weight, and fought for the same title, had the right credentials to become his trainer. So John and his brother signed up with London manager Dennie Mancini.

Eighteen straight wins, including eight stoppages inside three years, saw Feeney become challenger to the 'Welsh Windmill', Johnny Owen. Since becoming British bantam champion in November 1977, Owen had already become outright Lonsdale Belt holder, Commonwealth champion and European champion at the second attempt against Jean Francisco Rodriguez, the Spaniard being the only blot on his record. Owen's Commonwealth title was also on the line in a Wembley fight which was intended as a warm up for a world title fight with the Mexican WBC champion, Lupe Pintor. Feeney did well against a great champion, but Owen was tireless, swamping his man with punches. Feeney blocked and defended to a high order and threw some good punches himself but he struggled to match the champion's work rate. By the halfway mark Owen's strength was a big factor. The Welshman began to push his opponent around and, as the fight got to round thirteen, the only way the Hartlepool challenger could win was by knockout. With the fight in the bag, Johnny, still looking fresh, played safety first in the last round. Tragedy struck in Los Angeles three months later when Owen, knocked out by Pintor in round twelve, never recovered after being carried from the ring unconscious. Ring deaths always hit home more when the fight is at world title level and Britain lost a boxer who looked to have had the quality to be compared with the Welsh legends of the past like Jim Driscoll and Jimmy Wilde.

After keeping in the picture with three wins, which included victories over Terry McKeown and Steve Sims, who would later meet for the British featherweight title, John got his chance to fight for Owen's old European title. He was matched against the new champion, Valerio Nati, at Cervia in Italy, but the biggest night so far in Feeney's career ended in controversy. Feeney's short punches gave Nati repeated problems. The English fighter dropped the Italian with a left hook in round two and badly staggered Nati in round four. When Nati hit the canvas, the French referee took Feeney to a neutral corner before beginning the count, thus allowing the Italian an extra five seconds recovery before the count was started. In round four, when another left hook had Nati in trouble, the Italian sat on the rope while Feeney punched away, before the referee intervened. Dennie Mancini could not believe it. He insisted that, instead of cautioning Feeney, the homer referee should have given Nati a standing count. The Italian's strength helped him get over his early problems and he got the decision. Mancini maintained his man would have won in England, claiming that it was not enough on the continent to edge the rounds It was necessary to win them decisively. Nati did put the work in to win some of the rounds, but the Hartlepool contingent considered him to be an average boxer.

Feeney soon got over his Italian adventure when he became British champion by stopping stablemate Dave Smith, who had gone twelve rounds in an unsuccessful bid against Owen, in eight rounds at the York Hall in Bethnal Green. No one was more pleased than George Bowes who had tried for the same title and now had trained the champion.

After ending 1981 as British champion, the following year proved dismal for the Hartlepool bantam. An unknown Mexican, Adriano Arreola, out-pointed him to thwart any world title plans. The following month he was stopped for the only time in his career, when in pursuit of the second of Owen's old titles at the Sydney Opera House; Australian product, Paul Ferreri, winning by technical knockout in round thirteen for the Commonwealth bantam title. Feeney had never lost twice in succession and worse was to follow in his next fight – a second trip to Italy to challenge for the European title – against a new Italian champion, Guiseppe Fossati, who looked a better opponent than Valerio Nati. Once he had found his range, Fossati took immediate control and for a lot of the fight Feeney was under pressure. The Italian was not a known puncher, but John took a lot of punishment,

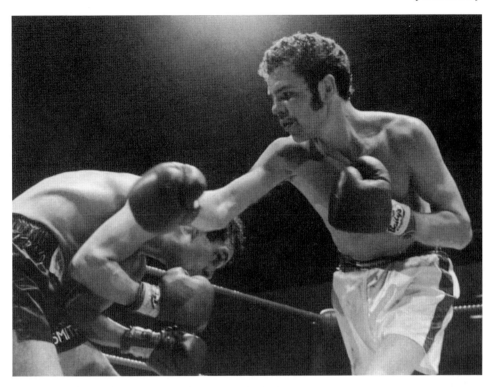

Dave Smith drops low against Hartlepool's John Feeney.

including a battering in round four when he went down. Feeney's courage kept him from going in the later rounds, when, knowing he could not win except by stoppage, he made a brave effort to pull things around. Fossati's winning margin was 120-110, 120-111 and 120-114. John returned home to end a disappointing year on a high note with wins over 'Kid' Sumali and Vernon Penprase.

Sixteen months after winning the title, Feeney made his first defence in what was the last British title fight to be staged over fifteen rounds and the first British championship fight to be staged at the Ulster Hall in Belfast. John was up against local hero Hugh Russell. The 1980 Olympic bronze medal winner had won all of his eleven fights since becoming a pro, including an eliminator against his Northern Ireland rival Davy Larmour. The much taller Feeney made his expected fast start and opened a cut above Russell's eye. The setback saw Russell box on the retreat, opting to dart in with quick bursts of punches. The Irishman had plenty of skill and with his ability to fluster the champion, he started to edge in front. Feeney was warned for head misuse in round five and after dominating round six, Russell appearing to lose interest, dropped his work rate. Feeney took round seven, as Russell's nose bleeding created another problem for the challenger. The Irishman's corner threatened to pull their man out unless he got back in the fight. Referee Sid Nathan threatened to do the same to Feeney after

Left: Programme for Feeney's 1986 British featherweight title clash with Robert Dickie.

Below: Italy's Valerio Nati hits the ground during the European bantam title clash with John Feeney, a fight which the Hartlepool man lost.

another careless head-butt. With the crowd behind him, Russell took rounds eleven and twelve. In the topsy-turvy fight, Feeney stormed back in round thirteen and, during a clinch, Nathan sent him to the corner for an alleged head-butt. Russell had taken his title on a disqualification ruling. Mancini's after-fight statement related that he had never seen such a prejudiced decision, adding that even the Irish wanted their man to win by the proper route.

Boxing returned to the Kings Hall in Belfast for the first time since the days of Freddie Gilroy and John Caldwell back in 1962, when differences between Catholics and Protestants were forgotten as two fighters from both religions took part in a British title fight. Russell's title reign lasted only thirty-six days, the shortest reign ever in the division, as Dave Larmour, who had turned thirty, became the oldest man to win the title when he out-pointed the champion over the new distance of twelve rounds. Larmour and Feeney had fought five years earlier, in February 1978, when the Irishman had come in as a very late substitute at Manor Place Baths. Larmour had protested bitterly when the referee had stopped it in Feeney's favour in round five. Larmour had not been off his feet and insisted he could have carried on. With time to prepare for the next occasion, Larmour had wanted a return with the Hartlepool man, and with Feeney his first challenger, Larmour had the chance to prove his point in front of his own supporters at the Kings Hall. Feeney had started the year as British champion and he finished the year back in the position. Larmour had lasted five rounds in the first meeting, this time John accomplished the feat in less than three. A tremendous left dropped the champion and referee Harry Gibbs was forced to end it when Feeney closed in to finish the fight.

Since his second attempt at the European championship, the title had changed hands again. The bad news was that the new holder was another Italian, the third in succession and the fifth Italian out of the last seven title holders. With his role as leading challenger, Feeney had no bones about travelling to a country where a knockout seemed the only way of winning. His third challenge for the title was at Campbasso three days after Christmas in 1983. There was no real complaint with this one, as the new champion, Walter Giorgetti, who floored Feeney in round one with an overarm right, ran out a twelve-round winner, which the judges saw 120–113, 119–112 and 118–115. It was a fight where John had struggled to make the weight. Having tested the water the previous year at Wembley, in a points win over Vernon Penprase, a move to featherweight was looking a more likely option. During the fight, the Italian had come out in round seven with eyes plastered with Nuskin, an illegal artificial skin. The French referee did not insist on its removal until the end of the round. Mancini claimed that had the fight been in England it would have been halted.

Amazingly, after three more point wins, including a result in Zurich against the former European featherweight contender, Sepp Iten, another bantam had surfaced from the Italian production line. In November 1984, a year since his last disappointment, Feeney was in Salerno for his fourth attempt at a title that had eluded him for four years. Feeney's luck had not changed and, almost predictably, the winner of the vacant tile was the Italian, Ciro de Leva, after twelve rounds.

The Gilbody's were the most successful brother combination in ABA championship history. George won four lightweight crowns (1977, '79, '80 and '81, future world champion Terry Marsh had won in 1978), while younger brother Ray had won the flyweight in 1979 and the bantam title in 1980 and 1982. George, who was expected to do well in the paid game, did not take the professional ticket and it was Ray, campaigning at bantam, with an unbeaten record of ten fights in just under two years, who was Feeney's opponent in his next British title defence. It was a fight John badly wanted to win. A win over the St Helens brother would not only give him the outright Lonsdale Belt, it would create history by emulating his own brother, George, who had recently achieved the feat. The other big factor was that the fight was at the Borough Hall in John's hometown. John had only fought as a pro in Hartlepool once before, but never as champion.

Feeney relied on his heavy punching in the early rounds, only to find that Gilbody was not only able to take his best shots, but carry the fight to the champion. Gilbody grew in confidence, but came crashing down to earth, when John's aggressive attack had the challenger reeling away with blood running down his face. Feeney's best rounds were six and seven, as Gilbody spent the six minutes concentrating on cover defence. John could not keep the pace and Gilbody, knowing he had to do it to win the fight, out-boxed the champion in the later rounds. Referee John Coyle saw it 117½–116½, although there was some surprise that the winning margin was not bigger. Feeney had the support but Gilbody had been his master. There was special delight for Gilbody's trainer, Gary Davidson, who had been in contention for the same title until eye injuries had lost him an eliminator. Manager Mancini, confirming that in future John would fight as a featherweight, thought that making the weight, which had become a problem for the defeated champion, had taken the edge off his fighter and had been the reason for his fading in the later rounds.

Feeney fought three times in the last three months of 1985: useful prospect Mark Reefer was stopped in three rounds, Kevin Pritchard a future super featherweight champion was out-pointed in eight rounds, and in December Feeney was back on his favourite hunting ground – Italy. The 1986 Olympic gold medallist, Maurizio Stecca, had put together an unbeaten run of eleven fights and, already well known in the country, Feeney was considered the ideal test in an eight-rounder at Casena. The jinx continued though as Stecca showed a great repertoire in his points victory. Feeney proved to be a dangerous opponent, but the future WBO world champion and two times European champion stayed on course to win a closely contested encounter.

Feeney's bantam pedigree had guaranteed him a high place in the British featherweight rankings and after only a handful of fights as a feather, John got the opportunity to become a double champion in the spring of 1986.

WBA champion Barry McGuigan had dropped both his British and European titles to concentrate at world level and with the logical contender, the unbeaten European champion Jim McDonnell, declaring no interest, John was matched with the relatively unknown Robert Dickie for the vacant title at the Royal Albert Hall.

The twenty-one-year-old Welshman Dickie, with only three years and thirteen fights experience (Dickie had won eight of his last nine fights and had won nine times inside the distance), was thought to have the punch to trouble Feeney. But the possibility of Dickie stopping a fighter who had forty-four fights behind him and had failed to go the distance only twice (one a disqualification in round thirteen and the other a stoppage in the same round in Australia), seemed remote. Debatable decisions had cursed John's career and in another fight he was convinced he had won, Dickie got the verdict by half a point. The fight kicked off at a blistering pace and Feeney's experience looked to edge him the early rounds as the overawed Welshman struggled to find his range. Dickie rocked Feeney in the seventh round with a couple of rights that had John stumbling and turning towards the corner post. Dickie followed up, but Feeney's craft averted the crisis and by the end of the round he had Dickie backing up. Dickie looked to have the better of the second half, but again it was difficult to score because Feeney rallied at the end of the rounds. While Dickie celebrated his title, George Feeney consoled a desolate brother who had lost his ninth out of eleven title contests.

Feeney's performance had earned a return and when John, now forced to fight in Ebbw Vale, got his title rematch later in the year, the new champion was going for an outright Lonsdale Belt. Dickie had knocked out former champion Steve Sims at the Ebbw Vale Leisure Centre and now wanted Feeney's scalp again to win his belt in 203 days, which would beat the previous record for the division, by Pat Cowdell, by a day. The second fight was much harder and John was the first to concede that a better man had beaten him, even raising the Welshman's hand in acknowledgement before the referee announced the official result. Referee Roland Dakin saw it 119½–114. In the opening round Feeney was down twice and in the next round it was John's turn to wobble the champion. It was the only time Dickie was troubled and with the Welsh crowd singing him to glory he demonstrated his champion qualities. Feeney, epitomising the true professional, finished with pride, making sure Dickie had to work to the final bell.

It was the Hartlepool man's last hurrah as a title challenger. There were two more fights in 1997 (a points defeat in London to Paul Hugging and a final North East appearance at Sunderland, where he out-pointed Nigel Senior) before Feeney bowed out of the sport with dignity. A pro's pro, it will be a shame if, in the future, he is only remembered for losing four European title fights in Italy.

George Feeney

Tuesday 12 October 1982 was a great night for North-East boxing. It was the night that underdog George Feeney stunned the Royal Albert Hall crowd by stopping the British lightweight champion Ray Cattouse, who had been unbeaten for five years, a feat that enabled George to celebrate with his brother John as the first family to hold British titles simultaneously. John had won his title just over a year previously and, although George's form had been patchy over the five years he'd been a pro, his determination helped make his first title shot a night to remember.

Born in Hartlepool in February 1957, George Feeney's amateur record was not anything exciting, although in an appearance for Young England he did out-point the German, Jorg Eipel, a future European welterweight champion. George turned pro under the guidance of John Spenceley, before eventually coming under brother John's manager, Denny Mancini. George Bowes, the evergreen of Hartlepool boxing became his trainer as George made his paid debut in August 1977, the month after John had made his first pro appearance. John won his second fight on the Stockton Fiesta bill and his one-year-older brother George made it a family double by stopping Eric Wood in four rounds. Four more wins followed, three of them in the North East, before the unbeaten record went to Tommy Davitt at the Anglo-American Sporting Club in Mayfair. It was Feeney's first ten-rounder and the razor-thin decision could have so easily gone to the Hartlepool man.

Mickey Duff managed the Uganda-born Cornelius Boza Edwards, whose career would take him to America and a WBC junior lightweight title, and who became the first of several past, present and future champions that Feeney would take the distance. Edwards out-pointed George at Wembley in September 1978 and the older Feeney spent the remaining years of the seventies competing against light-welters and welters.

George ended successive defeats with a second win over Eric Wood before dropping a points decision to Wolverhampton journeyman Bingo Crooks at Harrogate. The result warranted a return and in his next outing, Feeney gained revenge in Solihull and out-pointed Crooks – who, when retirement came, finished with more losses on his record than wins – again in a rubber match in Feeney's first fight of 1980. George ended the seventies with two wins in Glasgow. Scottish light-welter champion George Peacock went the distance, while Chris Walker, who had fought Colin Power for the British light-welterweight title in 1978, was stopped in eight rounds. Southpaw Clinton McKenzie was, for many, a boxer who never realised his full potential and challenged for a world title. Feeney gave the British light-welterweight champion a lively ten-round workout at Wembley in non-title action, before heading to Italy for the first of three career visits. In what was only his fifteenth fight, George was certainly mixing in exalted company; his thirty-year-old opponent, the Italy-based Argentinian, Juan Jose Giminez, had made an unsuccessful attempt at the WBC title against Leroy Haley only eight months previously. Giminez's experience had reached over eighty fights and fighting in a county that had the reputation of visitors only winning by knockout saw George lose by the inevitable points decision.

By now, brother John had already challenged for the British bantam title and the brothers' manager, Dennie Mancini, contended that George Feeney, who had spent the last eighteen months campaigning against quality light-welters, was good enough to challenge for the British lightweight title. Ricky Beaumont had revitalised boxing in Hull and George, used to fighting in opponent's backyards, had to contend with a lively home crowd in his eliminator for the lightweight title. The fight was a thriller and in the *Boxing News'* top ten fights for 1980. George lost by the narrowest of margins as Beaumont fired up by the crowd, with the edge in determination, hustled his way to victory. As it was, Beaumont lost his final eliminator to Scotland's Dave McCabe, who in turn was beaten by Ray Cattouse in Glasgow for the vacant title. Within six months, George had worked his back into another title elimination. Unbeaten with eight wins, Eddie Copeland had run out of preliminary grade opponents and his clash with Feeney at the Royal Albert Hall was the former amateur's step up to what was expected to lead to a British title fight. Copeland's hooks rocked Feeney early on, but the Hartlepool man carried enough experience not to be rattled. Keeping his composure, by round four Feeney had levelled the scores and with Copeland carrying a badly swollen eye his manager Terry Lawless pulled him out. In just over a month, George was back at the Royal Albert Hall fighting Winston Spencer – who apart from an unexpected loss to Teddy Carroll – was on a long sequence of wins, in an eliminator for Cattouse's title. Having got another chance in the elimination stakes, Feeney carried the perseverance and determination levels that had been lacking in his fight with Beaumont. Time and again he manoeuvred Spencer against the ropes or into a corner. For a time his opponent was able to worm his way out, but Feeney never let up and when George started to walk through his guard Spencer could not stop him and was punished accordingly, the referee rescuing Spencer in round ten. A title fight with Cattouse would come eighteen months later and in

George Feeney, one of two brothers, who kept the North East flag flying in the 1980s by becoming a Lonsdale six-belt owner at lightweight.

the interim period, Feeney completed two wins and suffered the only stoppage defeat of his career. John had boxed recently in a promotion in his hometown and George did likewise, out-pointing the Frenchman, Carlos Folder, in eight rounds at Hartlepool Borough Hall. George travelled to Lagos to fight the Nigerian lightweight champion and former world amateur champion, Davidson Andeh. George had problems with leg cramp and at the round-eight stage he was forced to retire, the only time in a defeat that the fight did not go the full course. In his fight before Cattouse, George met one of the sport's legends. Former world champion Ken Buchanan had been forced to abandon his retirement after a lengthy period and don the gloves again due to financial problems. Feeney had prepared for a final eliminator with Ricky Beaumont, but when the Hull puncher withdrew with a shoulder injury, Buchanan came in to take his place. The Scot showed all his old class in the opening round, but as the fight went on he could not compete with Feeney's work rate. George won the eight-round contest and Buchanan's comeback was over. His fight with George Feeney was his last.

In October 1982, George got his chance with the champion of the last two and a half years, Ray Cattouse, who himself was a boxing brother (five months earlier Trevor Cattouse had lost in four rounds in a tilt at Tom Collins' British light-heavyweight title in Leeds, which, of course, would have given the Cattouse family the honours that the Feeney boys were chasing). Unbeaten for

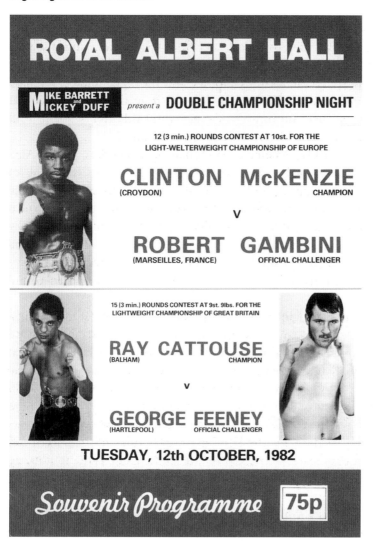

ROYAL ALBERT HALL

MIKE BARRETT and **M**ICKEY DUFF *present a* **DOUBLE CHAMPIONSHIP NIGHT**

12 (3 min.) ROUNDS CONTEST AT 10st. FOR THE
LIGHT-WELTERWEIGHT CHAMPIONSHIP OF EUROPE

CLINTON McKENZIE
(CROYDON)   CHAMPION

v

ROBERT GAMBINI
(MARSEILLES, FRANCE)   OFFICIAL CHALLENGER

15 (3 min.) ROUNDS CONTEST AT 9st. 9lbs. FOR THE
LIGHTWEIGHT CHAMPIONSHIP OF GREAT BRITAIN

RAY CATTOUSE
(BALHAM)   CHAMPION

v

GEORGE FEENEY
(HARTLEPOOL)   OFFICIAL CHALLENGER

TUESDAY, 12th OCTOBER, 1982

Souvenir Programme 75p

The programme for the fight that clinched the Feeneys' remarkable double. For the first time ever, two brothers held British titles at the same time.

twenty-seven fights, and needing the victory to clinch the outright Lonsdale Belt, it looked hard for the outsider to see beyond Cattouse retaining his title. The pundits agreed that stamina was going to be the deciding factor and most of them went for the champion, for stamina was one of his strongpoints. The pairing produced a ferocious battle and Feeney demonstrated his own brand of stamina to go with strength and punching power. Cattouse had not lost since his debut fight and showed tremendous bravery as the defending champion before he finally wilted in round fourteen. It had needed blood and guts to win the title and George Feeney had produced both to bring immortality to his family name.

It always hits home harder when a ring death occurs in a major title fight. Such a fight happened at Caesar's Palace in November 1982, when Korean Deuk

Koo Kim, who was challenging the WBA lightweight champion Ray 'Boom Boom' Mancini for his title, died four days later from his injuries. Unfortunately there were further fatal repercussions from the fight that had ended in round fourteen. Four months later the boxer's mother and the fight referee, Richard Greene, both committed suicide. Another follow-on from the tragedy was that the WBC decided to reduce the rounds of their world title fights down from fifteen to twelve and the other boxing bodies followed suit.

In Atlantic City in 1981, Mancini had challenged modern great Alex Arguello, the man who had taken Jim Watts' WBC title, before switching to WBA where, in three title fights, he had completed three inside-the-distance wins. Wanting to make a low-key return and to avoid the glare of the American media, Mancini's comeback fight was in the first week of the following January at St Vincent d'Aoste in Italy. Like he did against Clinton McKenzie and would do in his next fight against Howard Davis, George Feeney gave the world champion, whose only setback had been against Arguello, the ten-round workout he needed.

Three months after the Mancini fight, George was back in Italy fighting against another world ranked American in former Olympic gold medallist Howard Davis. Since Jim Watt had brought him to earth, when the American's unbeaten record had tumbled in Glasgow, Davis had put together an unbeaten run of nine fights. Davis was a comfortable ten-round points winner over George in San Remo. But a world title never came his way. He lost a split decision to Edwin Rosario in Puerto Rica for the WBC lightweight title in 1984 and, four years later, he fought Buddy McGirt for the IBF light-welter title and was taken out in only one round. A comeback after six years out of the game came to nothing in the late nineties.

Liverpool southpaw Tony Willis, the two times ABA champion and Olympic bronze medal winner, was the first challenger for Feeney's British title at the Regent Crest Hotel in London. The original fight date had to be put back when George contracted flu and the boxing brother proved he had not lost his edge during his eight month lay off when he finished Willis, whose pro career had only reached thirteen fights, in just one minute of round one. Willis was caught cold by a right-left-right combination and, after being floored for a seven count, the Liverpool youngster was wobbling on his feet when referee John Coyle ended his challenge. Willis protested angrily, but the opinion was that Coyle had got it right.

The next horizon for George was the outright Lonsdale Belt. Paul Chance had seriously thought of quitting boxing until an unbeaten run renewed his confidence and gained him a title opportunity in front of his own supporters at Dudley Town Hall in February 1984. Chance had drawn with Cattouse, who looked a shadow of his former self, and the Midlander went into the fight with a record of thirty-one wins from thirty-nine fights. For once, Feeney was the favourite and at the end of twelve rounds it was George's hand that was held up as the outright belt winner. Two fights later and George's career was over. He out-pointed Mickey Baker at Wolverhampton and in his last fight he failed to land the European title in Germany, when Rene Weller out-pointed him in Frankfurt. Eye injuries, which developed during the fight, meant that the Weller bout was to be George Feeney's last.

He was a late developer, who came out of the shadow of his younger brother, and, in terms of achievement, did the better of the two. George's fight with Ray Cattouse fully merits its place in history alongside the other all-British classics like Boon *v.* Danahar and Williams *v.* Taylor.

Billy Hardy

No one could seriously argue against the fact that Jack Casey, Tom Smith and Billy Hardy stand alone as Sunderland's most famous sons of the ring. It is always difficult to compare boxers from different eras, but there could not be a more defining example of the times. Where Casey, as one of the country's leading middleweights got one title chance in over 200 fights during the thirties and Smith was nearing 100 fights when he got his one title chance during the war, Billy Hardy took part in twenty-one title fights in under fifty appearances. Billy won fifteen and drew one of his twenty-one fights, claiming British titles at bantam and featherweight, and Commonwealth and European titles at featherweight. He was robbed of a European championship at bantam level in Italy and, in three unsuccessful attempts at world titles, he was unlucky to lose a controversial decision to arguably the best bantam in the world at the time, in front of his own Sunderland faithful.

Born in 1964 and the second youngest of fourteen, Billy Hardy started boxing at the age of ten. Joining the Hylton Castle and Town End Farm Boys Club, Billy's amateur career certainly was not ground breaking. He lost his first five fights and a third of his 150 total, but with the determination to succeed, he won the junior ABA title in 1981 and was the North-East Counties bantam champion in 1982–83. Keen to make boxing his career, Billy answered an advert placed by the London manager, Harry Holland, who was looking for fresh talent. Holland was impressed enough to give the young Sunderland boxer a year's contract and Hardy uprooted himself and moved to London.

Starting with eight straight wins, Hardy did well, but after a setback, in which he lost two of his next three fights (his last fight for Holland was a stoppage defeat by Costa Rican, Jorge Prentas), he returned homesick to Sunderland. With a pregnant wife and a career in the balance, Billy worked as an electrician's mate before advice from his old amateur trainer, George Ibenson, saw Hardy sign for Dennie Mancini, with George Bowes, still involved in the North-East scene, becoming his trainer. This was the right move and in less than a year under his new manager, he was fighting former Commonwealth flyweight champion Keith Wallace in an eliminator for the British bantam title.

His Mancini era kicked off with a points win over Ivor Jones at the Royal Albert Hall. Billy repeated the result in his next outing, also in the capital, at York Hall. Prior to the fight with Wallace at Alfreton, Mancini accepted an engagement in Italy to meet the former European bantam champion, Valerio Nati. The Italian had succeeded the late Johnny Owen to the title and was the first of six Italians who would hold the European title during the eighties. Nati was not quite the fading star he seemed and Billy was forced to retire in four rounds with an arm injury.

Merseysider Keith Wallace had been groomed as the eventual successor in British flyweight ranks to Charlie Magri. Wallace had come unstuck when he tried to add the European title to his Commonwealth. The Madrid born Frenchman, Antoine Montero, (who was succeeded by Magri), was the stumbling block. Wallace had quickly moved to reinvent himself in the bantam division with the hope of meeting bantam champion, Ray Gilbody. Both fighters went down before Billy stopped Wallace in round seven. Broken ribs in sparring had delayed Hardy's challenge to the champion and the Sunderland man had been out of the ring for eight months when he stepped in with Gilbody in the champion's home town of St Helens in February 1987.

The two boxers had a history. Gilbody had beaten Billy on the way to his third ABA title in 1982 (he had won the flyweight title in 1979, Wallace had followed him the next two years and Gilbody, moving to bantam, had taken the 1980 and 1982 titles at the higher weight). They knew all about the former Commonwealth Games bronze medal winner in the North East. Gilbody had taken the title from John Feeney twenty months earlier in Hartlepool. Feeney had helped George Bowes get Hardy's career on the right track and, like the Hartlepool brothers George and John, Ray and George Gilbody were an equally well-known pair of boxing brothers. Gilbody had followed his win over Feeney with an eight-round victory over John Farnell and now needed the Hardy win to secure his outright Lonsdale Belt. During 1986, Gilbody had twice lost in attempts at the European title. Ciro De Leva had out-pointed him in Cosenza, Italy, and then, in his fight before Billy, Gilbody had gone out in one round against Antoine Montero, the conqueror of Wallace. The Frenchman added the European to his previously won European flyweight title. It looked like Gilbody had not got over his one-round defeat in Paris. The champion was down four times in the first two rounds. Down again in the third, the referee had no alternative but to stop the action and raise the hand of Sunderland's first ever-British champion, Billy Hardy.

Billy had become a British champion and still had not fought as a pro in his native area. That was soon remedied and, after wins over Rocky Lawlor and Brian Holmes in the North East, Hardy's first defence, at the Crowtree Leisure Centre in Sunderland, saw another score settled against a rival from his amateur days. John Hyland, ABA bantam champion in 1983 and 1984 had stopped Billy en route to a final, a decision that the British champion had never accepted. Since turning pro the Liverpool southpaw had lost one from twelve. Cartilage trouble for Billy delayed

Sunderland's nineties hero,
Billy Hardy.

the fight and when Hardy returned after a nine-month layoff, there certainly was
no sign of ring-rust. It was unlucky thirteen for Hyland. He made the mistake of
trying to mix it and a left hook knocked him out in round two.

Vincenzo Belcastro was the latest Italian to hold the European title and the old
saying in boxing that 'the only way you can win in Italy is by knockout', which
had rung true in the sixties and seventies, prevailed in the eighties. In November
1988, Billy had his first European challenge at Fuscaldo and lost on points, and
in the following June Hardy was given a draw, which meant the Italian remained
champion. British boxing did get revenge on Belcastro in 1994, when the Italian,
in his second spell as champion, boxed out of Italy and was beaten in Sheffield
by a fast emerging Prince Naseem Hamed. It was the future world champion's
first title. In between the two fights in Italy and in the fight immediately after
the draw, Billy made title defences, which assured his outright Lonsdale Belt.
Glaswegian Ronnie Carroll, who would contest six titles and not win one, was
out-pointed in a close affair, while Brian Holmes, who Hardy had already beaten
on points, did not go past one round.

The scene was now set for Britain's longest serving champion to challenge for
world honours. Billy was now working as a swimming attendant at the Crowtree
Leisure Centre and the town came out to back him in full at the venue, which
had been the scene of his earlier triumphs, when he became the first Wearsider
to contest a world title.

Orlando Canizales was one of two brothers from Laredo competing at world bantam level. Two days before Orlando met Billy, the other brother, Gaby, failed to recapture the WBC version of the title, when he lost on points to title holder Raul Perez from Mexico. Orlando's manager Jesse Reid said during the press interview that he was pleased to fight in England as his man had suffered with opponents not wanting to meet him. Canizales, who held the IBF version of the title, came with good references as an aggressive fighter, who could box and use every angle. The American had turned pro in 1984, after an amateur record of 109 wins out of 120 fights. His only defeat had come in his flyweight days against Paul Gonzales, an Olympic gold medallist. Billy knew what it was like to box in somebody else's backyard (he would later box in Orlando's). Hardy was attempting to emulate Glenn McGrory, who had become the North East's first world title holder, when he had taken the cruiser title the previous June.

After his two raw deals in Europe, another controversial defeat was a bitter pill for Billy Hardy to swallow. After the twelve rounds Hardy, to great acclaim, raised his arms aloft in triumph only to hold his head in despair when the judges' points were read out and he found he had lost on a split decision. Billy had been cut on the left eye in the sixth round and forced to take a count in round nine. Canizales was never allowed an easy ride and took an awful lot of punishment, finishing the contest with a closed eye. After a six count in round nine, Hardy had responded brilliantly. He had a great round eleven, which he clearly won and many thought he had won the last round as well. The grandstand finish was not enough to convince judges Richard Murray from America and Walter Cavalieri from Italy: they judged it 115–113 to the champion. Britain's Dave Parrish seeing it 116–113 to Hardy. The American champion had underestimated Billy Hardy, who had been a massive underdog. Billy's performance was worthy of a rematch and when or if it came off, Billy knew he would be heading west.

Billy finished 1990 off with a technical knockout decision over the Mexican, Miguel Pequeno, at Thornaby Pavilion in Stockton and a British title rematch with Ronnie Carroll. The Glaswegian, only beaten by two points, had given Hardy his toughest title defence and fully deserved another tilt at Sunderland's finest. Billy beat him in eight rounds before the news of a world title rematch was announced. For his warm-up fight, Billy stopped Mexican and recent Canizales opponent, Francisco Ortiz in eight rounds.

In May 1991, fifteen months after their controversial first meeting in Sunderland (a fight that had been rated as the contest of the year in the annual British Boxing Awards), Billy Hardy travelled to the cowboy town of Laredo for his rematch with Orlando Canizales for the American's IBF bantam title. Six weeks were spent in preparation in South Africa, where Billy had a brother, and some time in Mickey Duff's gym in Florida, before he arrived in the border town of Laredo.

Canizales was not taking any risks having underestimated his challenger in the split decision fight in England. His Mexican ancestry had guaranteed a crossing

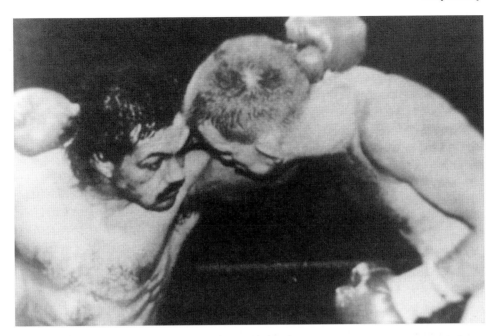

Above: Billy Hardy in action against world champion, Orlando Canizales, a fight in which Hardy nearly became the North East's second world champion.

Right: Double British and Commonwealth title-holder at bantamweight and featherweight. Billy poses with both belts.

of the borderline, for the Mexicans loved their fighting. Billy's share of the purse was 25 per cent, which was close to £7,000 after deductions. Fortunately a group of North-East businessmen had donated £4,000 towards his training and travelling expenses. Twice before, British boxers had found boxing in the open air in hot, stifling conditions with temperatures around a hundred degrees very much to their detriment. The elements played their part in both Colin Jones' and Barry McGuigan's defeats in Nevada. A crowd of 7,000 packed into the open-air arena in the grounds of the Laredo Civic Centre. This was the first world championship held in Laredo and Canizales did not want to let the home crowd down. He set a tremendous early pace and a tense Hardy was force to try and stay with it. Billy looked to be coming out of his traumatic start, when a left hook from the champion floored him for an eight count. He laboured for a couple of rounds and did well to win rounds six and seven. It looked like the humidity might be getting to Canizales, until he delighted his followers with a thundering left a minute into the eighth round. The blow lifted Hardy off his feet and he lay on the canvas for a full minute, before he climbed unsteadily to his feet. Hardy refused to blame the humidity for causing part of his downfall: 'I was beat on the night by a great champion, one of the best in the world. I'll cry now, but I'll be back.' Orlando was a great champion and held the IBF title from 1988 to 1994 before retiring undefeated.

Shock waves rang out in Sunderland when, only a month after his return from America, Billy, blaming a lack of motivation, announced that he was quitting boxing. Four months later, almost as sensationally, Hardy decided the hunger had returned and he announced a comeback. But there would be changes. He would manage himself and compete as a featherweight. His comeback fight was against Chris Clarkson at the McEwan Centre in Houghton Le Spring. Once Billy began to find his rhythm the end was inevitable and Clarkson's challenge expired in round five. Managing yourself at top level could be precarious and Hardy and Mancini, who still owned a share in him, were united on a three-year contract tied in with Mickey Duff.

In his last fight of 1992, Billy contested the vacant Commonwealth featherweight tile at Crowtree. Despite only eight fights as a pro the tall Ricky Rayner proved a stubborn customer. The unknown Australian put up a tremendous battle before Billy finally ground him down in round ten. In a match interrupted for four minutes by light failure, it was revealed later that Billy had boxed from round four with broken bones in his right hand. After a six-month recovery period, Hardy was back at the same venue for his first defence of the new title. Canadian-based Jamaican, Barrington Francis, was a previous holder, but had relinquished it after winning the world WBF title, which he had recently lost again after three successful defences. In his previous British visit, against Robert Dickie in Glasgow, Francis had been forced to retire in the last round with a dislocated jaw. There were problems at the weigh in, when Billy came in 2 pounds over for the 9 stone limit. He took the weight off in time, but there were shocks in round two when Hardy, down for a eight count, came up with a bleeding left ear. Billy had problems with the Canadian's longer reach, but came back stronger in the later rounds when Francis started to tire badly. The last couple of rounds' effort ensured the contest went Billy's way.

The early to middle nineties was a productive era for British fighters in the world featherweight stakes. Paul Hodgkinson (European title, 1989–91, world WBC 1991–'93) and Colin McMillan (world WBO, 1992) featured early in the decade and were soon to followed by Steve Robinson, who took McMillan's world title and Prince Naseem who, like Billy, had successfully moved up from the bantam division. There was already talk of Billy meeting Hodgkinson's conqueror, the Mexican, Gregorio Vargas. With four different world titles now available, Billy kept in the picture by winning the vacant British featherweight title against Alan McKay in a fight for which Hardy's Commonwealth title was on the line. The European Boxing Union nominated Hardy to fight the winner of the Hodgkinson v. Maurizio Stecca European title fight, but that fight never came off. Hodgkinson challenged for Steve Robinson's version of the world title instead and then retired after his defeat.

After the McKay win, Billy's only other fight of 1994 was a Commonwealth defence in the Sun City Bowl, where the South Africa champion from Soweto, southpaw Stanford Ngcebeshe, was beaten in twelve rounds. It was another African for defence number four, back in Sunderland early in 1995, where the tall Percy Oblitei Commey, who had lost in a title challenge to Colin McMillan three years earlier, was stopped in the penultimate round. Following a draw in Saint Quentin, France, against Fabrice Benichou in non-title action, the Commonwealth champion returned to France in a bid for the European title which had eluded him as a bantam. Mehdi Labdouri had taken the championship off the Italian, Stefano Zoff, and in defence had eclipsed Britain's world champion (at three different weights), Duke McKenzie. Hardy was the Frenchman's second defence and, after seven years of trying, Hardy finally brought a European championship back to Sunderland, when he outwitted the Frenchman over twelve rounds. Having fought in France and America in opponent's backyards, after his previous Italian experience a trip to San Remo was not exactly relished. Zoff was no easy picking; the Italian would crown his career in 1999 by collecting the WBA lightweight title. Hardy knew he had to be convincing to come home with a points win and he was just that. His victory threw out a strong challenge to the most exciting boxer in Britain of the time, WBO featherweight champion, Naseem Hamed.

The man whom Hamed had taken the world title off was Welshman Steve Robinson. Before his fight with the Sheffield boxer, Robinson had put together an impressive list of title victims, including the cream of British feathers, Paul Hodgkinson, Colin McMillan and Duke McKenzie. No one had stopped Robinson inside the distance during thirty-one fights and, in front of his beloved Welsh fans, he was thought to be invincible. That was until he met

Prince Naseem in title defence number eight in Cardiff. Robinson had mocked the twenty-one-year-old upstart but, if there was a lesson to be given out, Hamed gave it. In trouble afterwards for taunting the defending champion, the Yorkshire Prince made the Welshman suffer his first knockdown as he surrendered his title in eight rounds. After pondering his future, Robinson returned to the ring. After one comeback fight, eighteen months after his title loss in Cardiff, Robinson challenged Billy Hardy for his European title. Billy was looking for a world title fight showdown with Hamed, and he kept himself in front of the leading pack by making no mistake in out-pointing the Welshman. Although it was not known at the time, it was Billy's farewell appearance in Sunderland. Hamed, already well on the way to becoming one of the game's legends, although politics in the sport would not let it happen, was out to unify the featherweight division. Since his humbling of Steve Robinson, Naseem had acquired two of the four titles by beating the American IBF holder, Tom 'Boom Boom' Johnson, at the London Arena. The Hamed v. Hardy two-title clash was held at the Manchester Arena, three months after Billy's win over Robinson. In the morning papers on the day of the fight, Hamed predicted Hardy would go in one round. Billy responded by saying that he would not fall into the same trap as Steve Robinson; he had too much experience. Hamed was bang on the button. It was only ninety-three seconds into the fight and with the first real punch of the fight, Hamed's right saw Billy on the canvas. Rising at seven but still groggy, the thirty-two-year-old was a cornered mouse. A brutal left had him reeling again and with the writing on the wall, the referee decided he did not want to see any more. Although he might have had to swallow his pride, Billy was glowing in praise of his victor, expressing that he fully expected Naseem to take all four titles.

When he returned to the ring in 1998, Billy repeated his points win over Mehdi Labdouri, this time at the York Hall in Bethnal Green. By now there was another player fast bridging the gap to the top in the featherweight stakes. Scarborough's Paul Ingle was looking at Hamed and obviously saw Billy Hardy as the main stepping-stone in Britain. Ingle had already won both of Billy's old titles at British and Commonwealth level. Relinquishing his British title, the unbeaten Yorkshireman's Commonwealth title and Billy's European title were both on the line when the pair were matched at York in September 1998. Now aged thirty-four, Billy found it too hard to bridge the age gap. Billy, when the pair did box, looked the sharper, but was just worn down by Ingle's sheer persistence for which fitness played its part. By round eight, he could no longer keep Ingle at bay. Relentless pressure saw him fold and the referee put an end to a career of sixteen years in the professional ring. It was time to put away those famous red and white boxing shorts.

Glenn McGrory

The North East as always fetes its sporting heroes. Footballers and athletes are the usual headline dominators and although the area has produced some great boxers, it was not until 1989 that the Geordies could boast their own boxing world champion, Glenn McGrory. Three years earlier, after four successive defeats, the 6ft 4in heavyweight's career looked in tatters. A resurface in America gave him renewed confidence and a decision to compete in the recently introduced cruiserweight division brought the popular, good looking fighter the success he dreamed about as a youngster at the Consett Sports Club.

Born in 1964, from a big Irish family in Annfield Plain, Glenn's first boxing achievement was reaching the Northern Counties ABA light-heavyweight semi final in 1981. A junior ABA title and a Young England appearance followed before Glenn signed pro forms with Doug Bidwell, the father-in-law of Alan Minter.

Competing as a heavyweight and making his debut on the London dinner club scene, before returning to fight in local promotions, McGrory won his first thirteen fights. In the mid-eighties, the North East had two other heavyweights bidding for the top in Newcastle's John Westgarth and Hartlepool's Dave Garside. Westgarth's only defeat had come against Garside (a defeat he had avenged) and in Glenn's fifth appearance in Gateshead, the 6ft 5in Westgarth settled local supremacy when he knocked McGrory out in four rounds. Glenn returned to winning ways in his next fight, against Roy Skeldon, but then lost all his first four fights of 1986. Rudi Pika, who would later take his own life, and Anders Eklund (in Denmark) beat him on points and Garside at Blackpool and former British champion, Hughroy Currie, both stopped him. (Westgarth went the distance in an attempt to win the vacant European heavyweight title in Denmark against Steffen Tangstad in 1986. Later in the year Garside won his rubber match with Westgarth in a British heavyweight title eliminator. He was unsuccessful against the unbeaten Horace Notice for both British and Commonwealth titles and, at the end of his career, he joined McGrory in the cruiserweight division. Two of his last three defeats in the early nineties were to Siza Makathini, in an IBF intercontinental cruiserweight bout and Derek Angoi for the British and British Commonwealth cruiser titles.)

American Beau Williford, who had helped turn Dennis Andries from a journeyman into a three times world champion, had witnessed McGrory in the spar ring with Dennis and he suggested that Glenn would be better competing in the new cruiserweight division. Taking the excess weight off did the trick and the rejuvenated North-Easterner rebuilt his career in America under Williford's direction. Completing wins in Louisville over Joe Adams and in Houston, where he knocked out Calvin Sherman in the first round, McGrory returned in earnest to campaign for the British cruiserweight title. He stopped Andy Straughn, who had lost the title only a month earlier to Roy Smith, in Oldham, in an eliminator. But before he could fight Smith a chance came up to fight for the Commonwealth title in front of his own fans in Gateshead. The veteran Germany-based Zambian Chisanda Mutti had stopped another North East boxing hero, Hartlepool's Stewart Lithgo, to win the title three years earlier in Dusseldorf. Having lost twice to Lottie Mwale in attempts at the Commonwealth light-heavy title, Mutti, who held a verdict over Britain's Tom Collins, had twice contested the IBF cruiser title. At Monte Carlo in October 1985, against Lee Roy Murphy, after both boxers had gone down simultaneously in round twelve, Murphy came up to beat the count. Six months before his fight with Glenn, Mutti was again found vulnerable in round twelve, when American, Ricky Parkey, stopped him in Italy. Mutti's previous title defence had been in Australia, where he had beaten Dave Russell in Victoria. McGrory celebrated his first year as a cruiser by out-pointing Mutti for his first title and, in the first month of 1988, he challenged for the British title.

Tee-Jay, who had originally lost to Andy Straughn for the vacant title, had beaten Ray Smith in one round at Wandsworth to become British champion. At the same venue, with Glenn's Commonwealth title on the line as well, Glenn won his second title and, after a defence win over Lou Gent, Williford took him to America where he was employed extensively as a sparring partner to Mike Tyson. Further short-round knockout wins against Ron Warrior in Oklahoma City and Lorenzo Boyd in Metaine, Los Angeles, kept McGrory's name in the picture as a possible contender. Evander Holyfield held all three world titles, but when he decided to move up to heavyweight to challenge Mike Tyson, his titles became available.

McGrory got his chance to fight for the IBF version and was matched with the Kenyan born and now Swedish citizen, former world amateur champion, Patrick Lumumba. With the North East crying out for sporting success (Sunderland and Newcastle United were trying to recapture their former glories) the fight was put on at Stanley, near where Glenn hailed from. Normally the Louisa Centre held 1,500, but it was stretched to take 2,000, such was the interest. The venue could have been sold out five times over. McGrory had the locals off their seats when he almost did the job in the first round, as Lumumba struggled to survive a big left hook. Lumumba had to survive another crisis to stay the distance. Although tired at the end, the twenty-four-year-old McGrory was the overwhelming winner and new world champion.

Glenn McGrory, the North East's
first world champion, now a popular
summariser on Sky TV.

Another African, Siza Makathini, was the first challenger for Glenn's new
title, in October 1989. The fight scene moved over to a massive tent outside
the Eaton Leisure Centre on the outskirts of Middlesbrough, where promoters
Cedric Kushner and John Spensley were delighted with a full house of 3,500.
The IBF had ordered McGrory to defend against the American Jeff Lampkin in
December, but first Glenn had to see off an opponent, six inches shorter, who
carried a big punching reputation. Makathini had prepared in America at Brian
Mitchell's camp in San Diego. As he had to do in his title-winning fight, Glenn
had to work off a pound having come in above the 13 stone 8 pound limit.
McGrory entered the ring to a tremendous reception. By the end of nearly
twelve rounds, that reception had been well earned. The African's crouching style
and concentration on long punches to the body started to trouble McGrory in
the third and again in the following round. Makathini had definitely taken the
upper hand when, determined not to let his frantic supporters down, McGrory
started to turn the tide from round six. Sheer courage and a big heart got him
through the worrying period as the champion, on top in rounds nine and ten,
applied the finishing punches sixty-seven seconds into round eleven. McGrory
had taken the verdict and had shown champion's qualities to make it.

Three months later than originally planned Jeff Lampkin was the next opponent
in the North East and already there were cracks in Glenn's role as a cruiserweight.
He had created lots of interest in his native North East, but not outside, although

there were possibilities with the Lampkin fight because it was being shown in America. Making the weight was close again and the cruiserweight division was a long way behind the heavyweight division in the glamour stakes, which he expected to join again some day. Lampkin's record of twelve defeats from forty-six fights was not impressive for a title challenger, but in the last year he had won all his fights inside the distance. His best win had come as a light-heavyweight against the current IBF champion at that weight, Charles Williams. Nerves played their part in the opening round at the Gateshead Leisure Centre, but as McGrory began to get the feel of the ring, he produced the best punch of round one with a clean uppercut, which stunned Lampkin. The American had a reputation as a defensive boxer, but it was his concentration on body shots that started to pay dividends. A single left hook under the ribcage put McGrory down two minutes and twenty seconds into round three. Gasping, Glenn tried to rise at eight, but could not beat the count. His world title reign was over.

The defeated champion returned to the heavyweight ranks and in the following year there was a great chance to break back into the big time when he met Lennox Lewis, undefeated in sixteen fights, for the British and European heavyweight title at the Royal Albert Hall. The former Olympic champion had ended British champion Gary Mason's thirty-five fight undefeated run and looked to be on an unstoppable roller coaster ride to the world title. Glenn was only 10 pounds lighter but was unable to knock Lewis off track. After he had been floored twice McGrory was counted out in round two.

Before his retirement in 1993, there was one more crack at his old IBF cruiser title. For years professional sport had been barred in the Soviet Union and, as part of the awakening of the new Russia with its communist boundaries no longer existing, the first modern-day world title fight was staged in Moscow. The promotion, given the title the 'Storm of Freedom', was put on at the Prospekt Mitre Stadium in front of an audience with no affinity to the imported boxers – they appeared subdued and silent throughout. While Glenn challenged the current IBF cruiser champion Alfred 'Ice' Cole, the chief support on the billing was former European super middleweight champion Vincenzo Nardiello v. American Bruce Starling. The twenty-nine-year-old Cole, who had won twenty-one from twenty-two fights, was the third American in succession to hold the title following Lampkin, who had retired undefeated, and James Warring. As per usual, in all his world title fights, McGrory had to lose weight after the official weigh-in. He did extremely well in round six to avert a stoppage when his second trip to the canvas coincided with the bell. After his previous short-round defeats McGrory did well to last the course. He was never going to win his last hurrah; the judges gave it to Cole by in-between seven and ten rounds.

Since his fighting days, Glenn has worked in the boxing media, particularly as a member of the Sky TV team, where his inter-round summarising with commentating partner Ian Darke has become an integral part of the TV company's big fight nights.

Cornelius Carr

Able to boast Herol Graham, Henry Wharton, Michael Watson, Chris Eubank, Nigel Benn and Steve Collins, quickly followed by Richie Woodhall, Chris Pyatt, Robin Reid and Glenn Catley, the British middleweight scene was at its best ever from the late eighties into the mid-nineties. Cornelius Carr looked to be the natural successor to the likes of Benn, Eubank and Collins. But after beating favourite James Cook to land the British super middleweight title and giving the 'Irish Warrior' Steve Collins one of his hardest ever fights in world title action in 1995, it never really happened for the Middlesbrough-born fighter. It took time to get over the Collins fight and Carr even contemplated retirement. Appearances became spasmodic and Cornelius drifted back into six-rounders. There was a comeback to the limelight when he beat Salford's Steve Foster for the WBF world middleweight title, but when hand injuries failed to heal, Carr was lost to the fighting ring in 2001.

He was spotted brawling in the street at the age of eleven by trainer Marty Turner and by the time he was aged seventeen John (Cornelius) Carr had won a multi-nations bronze medal for England at Sardinia. In his last year in the amateur ranks, the Grangetown Club representative won the Northern Counties middleweight title and finished runner up in the ABA senior final. En route to the final, Carr beat Henry Wharton and lost in the final to Rod Douglas, who also did well in the paid ranks. Frank Warren, who by now had moved to the top of the manager/promoter tree in Britain, won the race for his signature and Carr made his pro debut in the second half of 1987.

Starting his career as a light middle, Carr made his debut at the famous York Hall in Bethnal Green and he halted Paul Burton in the penultimate round. When 1988 came to an end, the Middlesbrough newcomer's record read nine wins out of nine fights against carefully selected opponents, six of the victories coming early. Frank Warren got him to face plenty of experience in the opposite corner. Seamus Casey had gone past sixty fights and the Liverpool-based Franki Moro from Ghana had been in the ring with an array of champions: Kirkland Laing, Gary Stretch, Michael Watson, Chris Eubank and Chris Pyatt. Carr's first outing of 1989, in Reading, proved a shock, when the unfamiliar African Bocco George brought Cornelius down to earth, stopping him in three rounds. It was seven months before Carr was back in the ring. Welshman Carlo Colarusso was beaten in four rounds in his comeback fight and, during 1990, the Middlesbrough boxer fluctuated between light and super middleweight. Franki Moro was beaten again when Carr made his first pro appearance in the North. Moro took him the distance again at the Crowtree Leisure Centre and 'Corny' finished 1990 with two appearances in America. Both John Maltreaux and Jerry Nestor made their exits in round one. Returning to the North, Carr stopped Frank Eubanks at Thornaby and recorded a second win over Carlo Colarusso at Darlington's Dolphin Centre. Italy was the next stop and Brendan Ingle's Chesterfield ringman Paul Burton, who had gone in five rounds in Carr's debut, went in three in Verbania. In his second Italian fight, Leeds man Marvin O'Brien lost in round seven at Salemi. Cornelius was out of the ring for another year before he returned in October 1992 and, four victories on points later, with a record standing at twenty-two wins from twenty-three bouts, he made his first title challenge.

Just short of thirty-five years of age and with twelve years in the pro ring, James Cook was bidding to win an outright Lonsdale Belt. In a lengthy career the Jamaican born, Peckham-based middleweight had boxed thirty-four times, with twenty-five wins and nine losses, eight of his defeats coming in his first twenty fights. At Wembley in 1986, Cook had been the first man to beat Michael Watson. Herol 'Bomber' Graham who had just lost his aura of invincibility the year before, when his unbeaten record of thirty-nine fights tumbled to Sumbu Kalambay, came back to regain the vacant British middleweight crown by stopping the challenger Cook in five rounds. At twenty-nine years old, retirement looked a distinct possibility, but a five-round win over one time 'golden boy' Errol Christie, the boxer who look destined for the top, brought him into British super-middleweight title contention. When the chance came, he gave Irishman Sammy Storey a ten-round hiding in Belfast to become the champion at the age of thirty-one. Since then Cook had won and lost the European title and, after relinquishing his British title in a quest of possible world honours which failed to materialise once his European title had gone, he regained his old title in September 1993 by defeating the Brendan Ingle-trained Fidel 'Castro' Smith. Carr had never been beyond eight rounds and struggled for range in the opening rounds. Boxing cagily and preferring to stand off and concentrate on his left jab it looked obvious that the challenger was well prepared to go the distance against the older champion. At times criticised in his career for not following up a good start, Carr had got it right this time when he came strong in the later rounds. He floored Cook with a left hook in round ten and although the champion had enough left to win the last rounds, Carr stayed on course to become British champion by a point and a half.

The new champion never defended his crown. After another year out of the ring, he was back to business in 1995. With Britain comfortably off for world

Cornelius Carr, Middlesbrough's first British champion who gave the 'Celtic Warrior', Steve Collins, one of his hardest fights.

middleweight champions in the mid nineties, although he did not have the fight record pedigree in quality victims, Carr's name was constantly in the title frame during the year. Having abandoned his British title, he completed three routine point wins during the first half of the year. In what was expected to be the toughest of the three fights, Welshman Barry Thorogood was stopped in six rounds. And in what was his warm up for world championship challenge, Carr out-pointed the Germany-based Horace Fleary.

Cornelius had been the underdog in his challenge to James Cook and was very much in the same role when he challenged the 'Celtic Warrior' Steve Collins for his WBO super-middleweight title in Steve's home city of Dublin. It was a fight Carr eagerly took, despite only five weeks' notice and the fact that he would have to bulk up to super-middle to compete with the Irish strongman. Collins had won thirty times and his three defeats had all come in title challenges (Mike McCallum in the WBA title fight in Boston in 1990, Reggie Johnson in the WBA title decider in America in 1992 on a split decision and in Italy when he challenged Sumbu Kalambay for the European title). Collins had won the WBO middleweight title by stopping Chris Pyatt in five rounds in Sheffield and then had come his challenge for the WBO super middleweight title against the Chris Eubank, the man who was either admired or hated. Boxing fans prayed for Eubank to lose his title and Collins played the champion at his own game. He played an elaborate hoax and Eubank fell for it, believing Collins had been hypnotised to believe he could not lose. Collins took his title on points and when the two rivals met again, Collins won the return on a majority decision. Cornelius' fight with Collins was in Dublin on 25 November 1995.

Imitating Eubank, Carr entered the ring listening to a walkman to drown out the noise and refusing to let Collins, who let rip with taunts, intimidate him. Too much niggling prevented the fight from being a spectacle. Collins won unanimously, but his performance was laboured, untidy and disappointing. He never reached the heights of his Eubank performances and afterwards the champion's excuses were that that he could not 'get up for the fight', adding it would be a different story when he met Benn (Nigel Benn was in the audience and already plans were at an advanced stage to stage a unification fight with the WBC super middleweight champion in the style of the Benn *v.* Eubank extravaganzas). The Middlesbrough man never looked like pulling off a major upset, but he did display his own brand of 'Yorkshire grit' and stubborn determination. He found Collins with clean punches and solid counters and there was a lot of belief that if he could have stepped up in the fight's last quarter, when there was a chance to do so, the fight decision would have been very tight. When Collins had tried to move up a gear, Carr disrupted his rhythm, ensuring the champion's lead was never commanding. *Boxing News* compared the fight to the Nigel Benn *v.* Henry Wharton WBC title fight, a below-par champion against an inexperienced challenger unsure of his own ability to fight at the same level. Steve was not the only Collins to beat a Yorkshireman on the night. His brother Packy, conceding nearly a stone, beat former Carr opponent Marvin O'Brien. The Irishman's plans for a unification bout with Nigel Benn were thwarted when Benn unexpectedly lost to the South African, Sugar Boy Malinga, whom he had beaten four years earlier, on a split decision. While Malinga would eventually lose his title to Richie Woodhall, the Benn *v.* Collins fight came off later in 1996 for Collins' WBO title only. Benn had not been the same fighter since he had fought Gerard McClellan and in two challenges against Steve, he retired in round four with an ankle injury in the first and in his corner in round six in the return.

On the night that Benn lost to Malinga at Newcastle, Carr recommenced his career with a points win over Danny Juma. Throughout his career there had been lengthy gaps between fights and, after another lengthy period of inactivity, Carr returned with disastrous results. The Rivermead Leisure Centre in Reading, which had been the scene of his first defeat back in 1989, proved an unlucky venue again when the hard punching Dean Francis stopped Carr in seven rounds. Before the year was out, Francis, who had gone into the fight with Carr on the back of six successive knockouts, went on to beat David Starrie to clinch the British title before going on to add the European belt to his collection.

Cornelius had never had a big fight in the North and in February 1999 the opportunity arose when Carr was matched with Salford's Steve Foster for the WBF middleweight title. The week before there had been criticism over a WBF light-welterweight fight in Newcastle which was labelled farcical, when Junior Witter came in as a last minute substitute to win the title in two rounds. New promoter Gary Field, from the World Sports Organisation, was pleased with the turnout of over a thousand at the Thornaby Pavilion (above the central library) considering the fight was on Front Row pay-per-view television, in what was Thornaby's first ever world title fight. At thirty-eight years old and soon to be succeeded in the game by his son, Steve Foster, nicknamed 'The Viking', had retired a couple of years earlier after losing to Ronald 'Winky' Wright in a WBO light middleweight challenge. In his comeback as a middleweight, Foster, a pro since 1981, who had won twenty from thirty-seven contests (fewer fights than Carr), had lost to Howard Eastman in seven rounds in a clash for the British title. To show how much boxing has changed in recent years, the support fight to Carr featured Britain's leading female boxer, Jane Couch the 'Fleetwood Assassin'. Carr was sharp and impressive early on but seemed less effective in the latter rounds. There was no doubt that Foster was clearly out-pointed; the

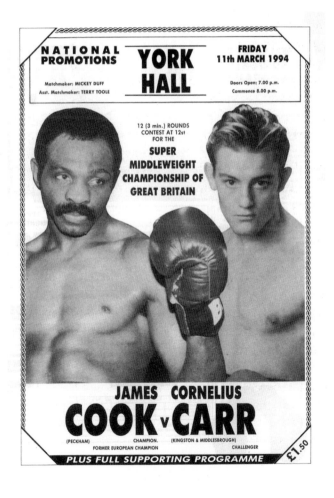

Cornelius' first title fight against James Cook at the legendary York Hall in Bethnal Green.

three British judges saw it 120–108, 120–109 and 120–110 in favour of the Middlesbrough man. Foster had tried to goad Carr in the later rounds, dropping his hands and taunting him that, despite his points lead, Carr could not knock him out. Carr refused to be drawn and ran out an easy winner.

Carr's first defence of his new title was against former world lightweight champion, Dingaan Thobela, well known in British boxing circles. In a career started in his homeland in 1986, the 'Rose of Soweto' put together an unbeaten record that saw him outgrow South Africa and find fame in the United States. He became the successor to the great South African legend, Brian Mitchell, when he won Mitchell's old WBA title against Tony Lopez in Sun City in 1993. Losing his title to the unbeaten Orzubek Nazarov, Thobela's form dipped when he was knocked out in eight rounds by the journeyman, Karl Taylor, and Geoff McGreesh in two rounds in England. At thirty, Cornelius was three years behind Thobela, who had done his training in solitude in a Soweto jail.

Carr was sharp and he made his punches count and an impressive points win against the former world champion looked to be the gateway to a possible tilt at one of the senior world titles (WBC, WBA, IBF and WBO). He signed a six-fight deal with the BBC, who were breaking back into televised boxing after giving Sky Sports a free run for the previous decade and a half. But damaged tendons in his right hand meant that he could no longer throw a serious punch and reluctantly he announced what would prove a short-lived retirement.

Thobela did go on to prove he was not a spent force in the top flight. In the following year he gained a crack at Glen Catley's WBC super-middleweight crown. Catley, strongly fancied to win, was well ahead on all three judges' counts, when the South African knocked Catley out with only seconds remaining in the fight. The popular champion lost in his first defence and moved up to campaign as a light-heavyweight after originally starting his career as a junior welterweight.

Carr decided to give it another go a year later. Gary Beardsley was a last minute substitute for Edwin Clearly in a four-round contest at the National Sports Centre at Crystal Palace in December 2000 and he made Carr work hard for his win. There was one more fight against the Australian champion, Sam Soliman, who had taken Neville Brown's Commonwealth title before losing it to Howard Eastman, who had also been touted as a possible Carr opponent until Cornelius' hand problems. Soliman won the six-round affair, the Middlesbrough man's career ending on his fourth defeat from thirty-eight fights.

Unlucky to be around when Britain had so much talent in the middle weight regions, the fights with Cook and Collins were the highlights of a career which promised much and was finally ended by his own hand injuries. More recently, Carr has been involved with training some of the Army's aspiring champions.

Michael Hunter

The North-East boxing capital title switched back to Hartlepool in 2000, when promoter and local manager Dave Garside's twenty quid Sunday afternoon shows, which included pie and peas, took off the at Seaton Carew Mayfair Suite. If the former heavyweight challenger Garside was looking for a star to pull the punters in to his shows, he quickly found one in super bantam Michael Hunter. Within four years and twenty fights, the former bricklayer had repaid the faith shown in him by his manager and trainer Neil Fannon, by becoming British champion and the first boxer from Hartlepool to hold a version of the world title.

Born in 1978, it was Michael Hunter's mother, with the notion of keeping her lad out of trouble, who took her son down to the Boys Welfare Amateur Boxing Club. Former world flyweight champion Charlie Magri, who certainly knew a thing or two about boxers from the lower weight divisions, tipped him as a future champion during his amateur days when Hunter completed the rare feat of winning two separate ABA titles (flyweight, 1997 and bantam, 1998). The year after his bantam title Michael chased a unique hat-trick when he unsuccessfully tried to land the featherweight title. Turning pro with Dave Garside and with Neil Fannon who had been with him in his amateur days as his trainer, Michael's debut came at Seaton Carew against another North-East lad, Sean Grant, in July 2000. By round three, Hunter was into his stride and, with the points win a formality, Grant did well to stay the course.

As well as Hunter, Garside was able to call on Kevin Bennett, himself a former ABA winner at light-welter and soon had other graduates from the Boys Welfare Club in Ian Cooper and Billy Bessey featuring in his shows. Chris Emanuele became the second Hunter victim when he survived two mandatory counts to stay the distance in Garside's second Sunday show. Darlington's Dolphin Centre saw Hunter outclass Walsall's Gary Groves and in his fourth win from four in 2000, Michael was in London to out-point Chris Jickell in a four-rounder. Back at Seaton Carrow, Huddersfield's Paddy Folan ducked and dodged Hunter all around the ring until Paul finally caught up with him in round five.

Journeyman Anthony Hanna, a veteran of over seventy fights, but with a draw and fourteen losses in his last fifteen contests, did not look much of an opponent for Hunter's next Sunday afternoon appearance at the Mayfair Suite. But the boxer, who had challenged Damian Kelly for the British and British Commonwealth titles in the nineties, gave the Hartlepool youngster a run for his money, before Hunter's sharpness edged the fight his way. The action switched to the Hartlepool Borough Hall a month later, when a return with Hanna was one of the support fights to a Richard Williams Commonwealth defence. There was disappointment on the night when Kevin Bennett, looking the most likely to be the first of the new breed to gain a British title fight, lost for the first time against Gary Ryder. Hunter won his fight. There was some alarm over the weight difference between the two fighters. Hanna had taken a fight the week before as a featherweight and had apparently lost 13 pounds in a week for the return fight and with Hunter coming in heavier after the weigh in, the weight difference was thought to be as high as 16 pounds.

Garside's Sunday afternoon show paraded house-full signs for the eagerly anticipated ten-round Northern Area super-bantamweight title clash with Sunderland's John Barnes. Experienced Barnes had fought twenty-five times, won twelve and had been in the ring with some good men, including Nicky Cook and Jason Booth. This, in comparison to Hunter's seven fights in just over a year, was expected to tip the result in favour of the Sunderland boxer. It was a big test for Hunter and while perhaps some thought the fight was too early in his career, he came through it with flying colours. He not only collected his first title as a pro, Michael became the first man to stop Barnes from going the distance. The Sunderland boxer had started the better, but once Hunter had upped his work rate, he began to look the stronger as the fight went past the middle rounds. The end came in round eight, when, with Barnes on the ropes, the referee decided the pressure was enough to end it. Barnes' people questioned the decision and indeed the round was only seconds away from ending, but even the die-hard Barnes supporters could not deny that Hunter deserved his glory. Hunter was back at the Mayfair Suite in November for his last fight of 2001. Substitute Joel Viney, who had won two from nine, could not cope with Michael's pace from the beginning and, after his man's one-sided points win brought a second successful year to an end, Garside announced that he was pushing his man for a British title eliminator.

A second excursion down south, on the same bill as Kevin Bennett, saw the Irish southpaw Steve Quinn lucky to survive the opening round. Hunter's half a stone weight advantage was a factor and, with nowhere to hide, Quinn was knocked out in the next round, as Michael's tenth successive win produced his first knockout. The fist blip on the Hunter record came in Michael's next outing at Crawley Leisure Centre where Marc P. Callaghan held him to a draw. It was a result the Hartlepool super-bantam did not take well and he was criticised in the press for a show of petulance: Hunter thought he had done enough to clinch

Hartlepool's British super-bantam title holder – the North-East's latest champion.

the fight in the last round. There was a chance to reach a larger audience when Michael and Kevin Bennett fought on the Naseem Hamed comeback fight undercard at London Docklands. (Hamed was fighting Manual Calvo and others on the bill were Michael Brodie, Colin Dunne and Wayne Rigby.) With one loss to British featherweight champion Dazzo Williams in fifteen fights, Coventry's Michael Payne was never going to be a pushover. While Kevin became Colin Lynes' eighteenth successive victim, in his hardest fight yet, Hunter put himself in title contention with an impressive eight-round win.

With what one might label a second division of world titles appearing on the market (i.e. IBO, WBU and WBF), Michael's unbeaten record enabled Dave Garside to forward him as a candidate for one of the newer titles. It was not hard to sell tickets for a world title fight in Hartlepool and the promoters made brisk trade for Hunter's challenge for the vacant WBF super bantam title at Jesters Leisure centre in Hartlepool. Michael's opponent, Frankie de Milo, had an unusual history. Born in Rwanda, he had fled that country at sixteen after being shot in the back. Settling in Sweden he began a boxing career, signed with Chris Sanigar in 1999 and boxed out of England. In his fight prior, de Milo had lost in Copenhagen to Jadgar Abdullah. It was thought de Milo's phenomenal work rate might be a problem, but in the end the African Swede was reduced to arm smothering spoiling tactics to keep 'Hunter the Hunter' at bay. With the big crowd behind him almost to a man, Michael's harder punching finally put de Milo down in round seven. Over eagerness spoiled an early finish and Hunter's opponent had to be given praise for lasting the twelve rounds. It was a great fight, but there was only one real winner, the three judges seeing it 118–110, 119–110 and 118–111. Hartlepool had its first world champion, but Michael did not hold the title for long, relinquishing it to go for what was, in his eyes, the more prestigious British title.

Journeyman Michael Hanna was back for Hunter's next outing: another chance to shine for a larger audience. Boxing was back in fashion in Newcastle with a promotion that saw Ricky Hatton and Joe Calzaghe both fighting Americans and Alex Arthur in a title defence at Newcastle Telecast Arena. Hanna, heavier than the last time, had not won in his eight outings since his second fight with Hunter. The Hartlepool fighter won confortably in what was really only a contest marking time. The winning extended through 2003, with two point wins and two technical knockouts. An appearance in Trieste saw the Italy based Serbian, Afrim Mustafa, after a standing eight count, stopped in round five. In further journeys to the south of England and Northern Ireland, Rocky Dean went in one round in Plymouth and the Russian, Nikolai Eremeer, was out-pointed in Belfast. There was a magical night down at Bridgend in Wales, when Kevin Bennett became a true boxing hero. Battling exhaustion in the latter rounds, Kevin's guts enabled him to beat Michael Muya to land the Commonwealth lightweight title. On the same bill, Hunter's height and reach advantages helped him win over the Ukrainian, Guennadi Delissandra.

Hartlepool's boxing champions from the eighties, George and John Feeney, were both in attendance at Borough Hall in April 2004 when Michael challenged for the vacant British super-bantam title. John was seated in the audience while George was part of the team in the local challenger's corner. With home advantage and having previously beaten his opponent, Mark Payne, Hunter carried the favourite's tag. Payne had given the unbeaten twenty-five-year-old his hardest fight and, with the experience in his team, there was no way Hunter was taking Payne lightly. The Coventry boxer had beaten Marc P. Callaghan, the boxer who had spoiled Hunter's 100 per cent record in his warm up fight. Hunter could not fail to be fired up with his local backing and soon got into a cracking pace that Payne found hard to live with. As the rounds passed by, Payne could not keep his man at bay and all the advantage was with Hunter. The result was starting to look a formality when Mickie Vann, the Leeds referee with over 100 world title fights to his name, halted proceedings in round seven. The result enabled Michael to join the select band of Jack London, Teddy Gardner and George and John Feeney in bringing British titles to Hartlepool.

Garside does not think that Hunter will stop at a British title and, as the next stage in his progress, has a European title in his sights.

Bibliography

For King and Country by Brian Hughes: Collyhurst and Moston Lads Club, 1999.

Jock McAvoy: Portrait of a Fighting Legend by Brian Hughes: Collyhurst and Moston Lads Club, 2000.

Jackie Brown: the Man, the Myth, the Legend by Brian Hughes: Collyhurst and Moston Lads Club, 1996.

Byker to Broadway by John Jarrett: Bewick Press, 1997.

Hall of Fame by John Jarrett: Tups Press, 1999.

The Wearside Champions by Harry Potts: Bewick Press, 1993.

Jack London the Forgotten Champion by Archie Potts: Bewick Press, 1997.

Len Harvey Prince of Boxers by Gilbert Odd: Pelham Books, 1978.

Hartlepool Pro Boxers 1945–55 by Robert Smith: Printabilly Publishing, 1993.

Johnny the Story of the Happy Warrior by Alan Roderick: Heron Press, 1990.

The English Boxing Champions: 1872–1910 by Bill Matthews, 1990.

Linament and Leather: 60 years of the Fight Game in the North by Frederick C. Moffatt, 1982.

Claret and Cross-buttock or Rafferty's Prize Fighters by Joe Robinson: George Allen, 1976.

Jack Casey: the Sunderland Assassin by Archie Potts: Bewick Press, 1991.

The Heavyweight Championship by Nat Fleischer: Sportsman Book Club, 1954.

Two Fists and a Fortune by Bruce Woodcock: Hutchinsons Stanley Paul, 1951.

Jack Solomons Tells All by Jack Solomons: Rich and Cowan, 1951.

Twenty Years by Freddie Mills: Nicholson & Watson, 1950.

Refereeing 1,000 Fights by Eugene Corri: C. Arthur Pearson, 1919.

Life's a Knockout by Charlie Rose: Hutchinsons, 1953.

Recollections of a boxing referee by Joe Palmer: John Kane Bodley Head Ltd, 1927.

The Fight Game by James and Frank Butler: Sportsman Book Club, 1956.

Knuckles and Gloves by Bohun Lynch: W. Collins & Sons, 1922.

How to box six rounds by Spike Robson: Ewart Seymour and Company.

The Manchester Fighters by Denis Fleming.

Articles by Fred Charlton (on Jack Casey); southern ex-boxer.

Articles by Owen Moran (on Mickey McGuire, Tom Smith, Benny Sharkey and 'Seaman' Tom Watson): *Box On* London ex-boxers.

My Two Fights at Liverpool with ex-World Champion Freddie Miller by Billy Charlton: *Box On* London ex-boxers.

Various North East reports from John Jarrett: *Boxing News*.

Boxing Venues in Newcastle and Sunderland prior to the Second World War

By kind permission of boxing historian, Miles Templeton.

NEWCASTLE

Barley Mow Inn
Barrack Road Gym
Brough Park
Byker Professor Burnett's Saloon
Cambridge Hall
Newcastle Circus
Clayton Arms Saloon
Crown Electric Theatre
Drysdale Hall
East End
Elswick Theatre
Festival Hall
Gaiety Theatre
Ginnetts Circus
Gosforth Dog Track
RFA Gymnasium
Rokeby Arms
Royal Picture Hall
The Close Boxing Saloon
Trafalgar St Club Room
Victoria Running Grounds
Grapes Inn
Hexham House
Marlborough Crescent
New St James Hall
Nichol Brady's Gym
Nichol Brady's Gym – Half-Moon
Nichol Brady's Gym – Mechanics
Old Dolphin Hall
Oxford Music Hall
Palace Theatre
People's Theatre
Percy Cottage Saloon
Plimsoll Hotel
Newcastle Private Rooms
Queens Theatre
St George's Hall
Newcastle St James Hall
Newcastle St James Park
West End
Volunteer Artillery Drill Hall
White Horse Inn

SUNDERLAND

Arcadia Amphitheatre
Assembly Rooms
Drill Hall
Fulwell Club Grounds
Golden Lion Saloon
Hendon Running Grounds
Sunderland Pavilion
Sunderland Holmeside
Hudson Street Skating Rink
Sunderland Miners Hall
Professor Moore's Pavilion
Star Music Hall
Warehouse in Pann Lane
West End AC
Will Cameron's Booth
Old Hendon Running Grounds
Lambton Gym Club
Tantobie in field behind Commercial Hotel
Sunderland Royal
Tent